Dinner with Juliet

Dinner with Juliet

THE STOCKBRIDGE RESTAURANT COOKERY BOOK

JULIET LAWRENCE WILSON

with photographs by Alan Donaldson

LOMOND

First published in Great Britain in 2002 by

LOMOND

36 West Shore Road

Granton

Edinburgh EH5 1QD

Text © Juliet Lawrence Wilson

Photographs © Alan Donaldson

Design by Creative Link

© Lomond Books 2002

All rights reserved

A catalogue record for this book is available from the British Library

ISBN 1 84204 054 5

Printed in Scotland by Bath Press Limited

ACKNOWLEDGMENTS

**This book is dedicated to Anne
and Lawrie Wilson.**

I would like to thank everybody at Lomond Books, especially Mary Keegan for her
enthusiasm and help with the book. Writing it has been a great experience, not to
mention therapy! Many thanks for giving me the opportunity.
Thank you to Alan Donaldson for your amazing pictures, endless creativity and being
such a pleasure to work with.
To Karen Fitzpatrick for her saintly patience and her editorial attention to detail.
To everybody at Creative Link.
A big thank you to all the staff at The Stockbridge Restaurant.
Thank you to all my suppliers.
Many thanks to G. Armstrong, fishmongers.
To Sarah Dalkin at Jeremy Hicks Associates.
To all my regular customers, you have all been a pleasure to cook for!
Most of all, I would like to thank my wonderful parents for their love, encouragement
and support. For helping out, above and beyond the call of duty, for keeping me sane
and the plants alive. I love you both so much and I couldn't have done it without you.

FOREWORD

Walking down the well-trodden steps to the Stockbridge Restaurant you have the impression of going to a private dinner party. It is not just the warm welcome, the flattering candle-light or snug comfortable seats, it is also the fact that the personality of the cook is so evident in the food. From the chic home-cured salmon through gutsy, robust venison then hip vodka sorbet and finally comforting steamed mango pudding, this is food with a highly personal touch. It is not soulless food cooked by a band of chefs remote from customers ; this is, indeed, Dinner with Juliet.

The recipes in this, Juliet's first book, are clear, concise and appetising. None have long lists of exotic ingredients or complicated methods that those living in a chef-free zone could ever attempt. They are straightforward without being mundane, for this cook's food is delicious yet somehow out of the ordinary. It is flamboyant but with its feet firmly on the ground. There is a highly personal feel in her recipes, as there is in her restaurant food.

What I also appreciate, as one who is forever writing about the importance of sourcing locally wherever possible, is that Juliet uses Stockbridge for her prime ingredients. She describes herself as The Bag Lady of Stockbridge as she trundles along Raeburn Place with her bag full of seafood from Armstrongs the fishmonger or pheasant from Bowers the butcher. And since I have also bought my fish and game from those two shops for many years, I could be accused of being slightly partial. And probably I am, but I can assure you there is absolutely no questioning the quality of their produce.

For those of you not fortunate enough to dine with Juliet at her restaurant, I commend the recipes in this book to you. Does a bowl piled high with mussels cooked with cream, wine and saffron not set your gastric juices running? Or what about a plate of home-cured wild salmon with wonderfully crisp home-made oatcakes? If not, what about the famous Game Terrine with onion marmalade? I say famous as, the last time I ate at the restaurant Juliet had advised me in advance the terrine would be on the menu. On arrival, it was not. She told me later she had dropped the entire terrine dish on the floor that afternoon and so improvisation was called for - and a quick whiz around the delis of Stockbridge saved the day. Which is more than can be said for that glorious game terrine, which I was amazed to see - freshly made! - on the menu again the following week. Lesser cooks might have been put off for ever.

Main courses might be paella with sangria, posh fish and chips or duck with berry sauce. Or of course the perfectly timed venison en croute that I enjoyed one summer night. Because Juliet is not professionally trained, it is perhaps more reassuring for us, non-chefs. We might not be able to cook for forty-five covers a night but we could certainly recreate the dishes in our kitchen with apparent ease.

Puddings are hearty and gutsy, as befits the requirements of Juliet's fellow Scots. Chocolate and stem ginger pudding with white chocolate sauce or mango and pineapple steamed pudding are perfect in winter or summer. For do not forget that in Scotland, warm, comforting puddings are not seasonal.

What is also interesting about reading this book is the author's own story - the ups and downs of restaurant life, from taking over and renovating premises to the day-to-day running of the establishment; and caring for customers who can range from — in the author's words 'the loveliest people in the world' to the 'spawn of Satan'. I have been there on a night when a 'tricky' crowd were in,

yet there was no fuss or bother. It was all dealt with and Juliet emerged from the kitchen smiling, as if it had been just another day in the life of your neighbourhood chef.

And that is what it is all about: maintaining a consistent flow of dishes (or recipes) to please customers (or readers) while keeping a firm sense of reality. A sense of humour is a prerequisite and that is evident in this book. Once you have read the story, read Tips for Successful Cooking on page 188 and follow these recipes to the letter and you will enjoy dinner with Juliet in your very own home.

Sue Lawrence

SUE LAWRENCE, AUGUST 2002

contents

Once up

on a time

LIKE ALL GOOD IDEAS, THIS ONE TRANSPIRED IN THE PUB I'LL OPEN A RESTAURANT.' AT THE TIME THERE SEEMED NO REASON NOT TO.

dinner with juliet

ONCE UPON A TIME

ike all good ideas, this one transpired in the pub. 'I think I'll open a restaurant.' At the time there seemed no reason not to. If only I had said, 'I think I'll become a criminal mastermind or a spy.' Never mind, there are worse avenues for one drink too many to take you. Unlike most of my bright ideas that occur under the influence, this one didn't seem too bad in the cold light of the morning after. I could cook, I could organise and if restaurateurs have to have drink problems, I was already half way there.

At the time I was a perfectly happy outside caterer. People said that I catered for the rich and famous of East Lothian — a myth I continued to perpetrate. In reality it was a dream of a business to run — few overheads, lots of work but plenty of time off if I wished. The best thing about outside catering is that people are generally employing your services for a special occasion and are particularly appreciative for the extra trouble that I would go to. The only thing I didn't like about outside catering was that I would deliver the food and seldom get to see people enjoying it. It was a Cinderella lifestyle and I have always been the kind of girl that wanted to go to the ball. The only other bad thing was that it was very solitary work and I got to the stage that when the Jehovah's Witnesses came to the door I was welcoming them in with open arms.

I had a passion for cooking from a very young age. When I was little I used to help my grandmother with her Saturday morning baking extravaganzas. Most of the results would be dispatched to the nearest conservative ladies coffee morning but there would be plenty left over for 'elevenses' when gran would wheel a trolley into the living room full of the most amazing cakes and scones. Gran would then tell us about all the people who had died (the obituary columns being akin to *Hello!* or should that be *Goodbye?* magazine for my grandmother). She would send us off with a basket full of jams and baking. I still love baking to this day and when I do bake, I can't help but think of the merits of a co-operative funeral service.

I had gone into catering as a way of earning some extra money. I had previously wanted to be an actress and when I look back at that stage of my life, I now realise that I actually did quite well. The most unusual aspect of my C.V. was that I was the only Scottish member of equity never to have been in Taggart — even as a corpse. Yet I had become disillusioned with the lifestyle and most of all with the other people involved in it. Actors tend to be a breed unlike any

IN THOSE TWO YEARS I CAME TO REALISE EXACTLY HOW NAIVE I WAS.

other. The luvvie stories that you hear are not far off the mark. I just couldn't get into the air-kissing thing. My main downfall however was the inability to be completely and utterly obsessed with myself.

I should have realised it was all a waste of time when I was at drama college. We were doing an exercise where we had to pretend that we were aliens hatching from eggs. My tutor told me that he didn't believe in my egg. That would have been because the egg wasn't b***** well there, I wasn't an alien and none of us lived on Mars. Eggs form a large part of my life now and goodness knows I appreciate the reality of them.

The dressing room conversations were always the most difficult to bear. People who work in the arts would have you believe that riches and fame do not

matter as long as you are working with good material. I don't really buy this: show me an actor who doesn't want to get to Hollywood and I will show you someone who needs his or her head examined.

Acting wasn't for me. My career came to an end when I was cast in a short film as a gun wielding lawn-mower mechanic. I still reach for a paper bag to cover my head whenever I think about it.

My mind was made up: I was going to become a restaurateur. The first thing was to find a unit, an empty space that I could turn into a restaurant, or an existing restaurant. Now you might think that the process from idea to result would not take that long. I thought that once I had found my location I could be open within six months. In reality it took two years. There is absolutely no need for this long time scale because if every body got their act together it could be a great deal shorter and easier. It's simply the way things work. In those two years I came to realise exactly how naive I was.

Very early on I had completely fallen in love with my dream premises. It was only two empty old shops with rising damp and dubious floors and ceilings but I could visualise its potential. It was in a lovely area of Stockbridge near to the old market arch and surrounded by classy designer shops. I had a suspicion that there might be some competition to get it. This was not because the sleeping bag and clothes on the floor indicated that a squatter had been living there.

The property market was buoyant and properties were being snapped up. I decided to take the bull by the horns and arranged a meeting with the estate agent to try and find out exactly how much money the landlord wanted for the lease. At this point I was prepared to offer three thousand pounds over the asking price as I felt that the property was worth it. Luckily for me the estate agent told me that the landlord would be perfectly happy to accept three thousand pounds under the asking price. I had managed to save myself six grand a year and got the

unit I wanted. Unfortunately, not everything was this simple.

Step two was to get the lease sorted out. I have often thought that if they taught us to do this kind of thing at school then we wouldn't need lawyers. Similarly if they taught us to cut our own hair we wouldn't need hairdressers. Thank goodness not everybody at school takes cookery lessons or I would be out of a job and have no chance of ever finding a husband. The process of negotiating a lease is notoriously long and slow. I had a good lawyer but no matter how efficient your lawyer is, this is the way the legal system works and there is nothing that either of

you can do about it. Missives are exchanged back and forth as if paper is going out of fashion and the costs are huge. Luckily, my lawyer was a handsome, dashing chap, which made the tedious meetings less of a chore. There is no point, however in trying to come across as an Alexis-from-Dynasty type to try and get things moving quicker — that kind of stuff only works on the telly.

Similarly my frustrations escalated when dealing with the council planning department. A lot of council departments are like fairies in that you know they exist but never see them. I found that getting someone from the planning department down to look at the restaurant was impossible. I am sure it is not their fault — perhaps daylight takes away their powers. Any sensible person might think that these authorities are in place to help and assist a small business person, after all, if they get empty units filled, the income from rates bills is higher, the area is more vibrant, employment is increased and, all in all, everyone is a winner. The reality is somewhat different. Once again the process of getting anything done is notoriously slow. Often they will not deal with you in person and will only talk to an architect, which causes more expense. My general feeling was that they were reluctant to go out of their way to help you. If they had been able to override the bureaucratic structure, a whole lot of time, money and general aggravation could be saved all round.

The biggest mine field, however is finance. The days of going to a bank manager with a good idea and a business plan and getting a decision there and then because the individual you are dealing with believes in your project are sadly long gone. Nowadays everything goes through a committee who has never met you. I have had four different bank managers since I opened the restaurant and haven't met one of them. It sounds unbelievable but one financial institution asked me if I had a live-in boyfriend. When I inquired why this was any of their business they replied that the live-in bloke would be able to help me out if the business was going down the tubes. They obviously have more faith in the male population than I do. I don't have a live-in boyfriend but what there would be to stop him running off with a floozy when my business went into the doldrums — I don't know.

I had a pretty hard time convincing them that I had no intention of opening a restaurant to then decide to get married and start a family six months down the line. Perhaps I should have signed a statement saying I was an infertile lesbian and they might have given me more money. My own investment came from money I had saved from the catering business, shares that I owned and money that I had inherited from my grandmother. I had expected the bank to lend me the same amount but they would only lend me 10 per cent of what I had put in. With the work I was going to do on the property I could have sold the lease at a premium and recouped every penny, even without trading for one day. I also owned my own flat but they wouldn't take either of these things into consideration. I am sure that you have seen the adverts and read the literature. Banks love to portray themselves as institutions that help the small businessperson. Whatever! Call me bitter but sometimes I think that British banks make Shylock look like Florence Nightingale.

Through this period of time I genuinely felt severely hard done to. When you have a dream of owning your own little venture all you want to do is get on with things. Sitting, twiddling your thumbs while your confidence and bank balance is rapidly deteriorating is totally disheartening. I know now that you simply have to bite the bullet and hang in there. A regular supply of alcohol helps, preferably taken by an intravenous drip.

All these problems were frustrating at the time but were a picnic in the park compared to getting the physical work done in fitting out the restaurant. The unit I got had been empty for years and was split in two by a brick wall that had to have an archway knocked through it – hence all the palaver with the planning department. One half of the unit had been a feng-shui centre and the other half a tarot card reading shop. Funnily enough there was no note on the wall saying that there would be a restaurant here one day. Some of the customers think that the restaurant has a good Karma and after a few glasses of wine I believe them. There was no ventilation, floors, toilets or kitchen. Everything was to be started from scratch.

PERHAPS I SHOULD HAVE SIGNED A STATEMENT SAYING I WAS AN INFERTILE LESBIAN AND THEY MIGHT HAVE GIVEN ME MORE MONEY.

dinner with juliet

The contractors were hired and work finally started then suddenly stopped. The contractors seemed to have a problem turning up although sometimes they did turn up but left again. Arguments were had, promises were made and a few more jobs were done and then once again things came to a standstill. Needless to say they got sacked from the job.

It was a big risk but I had to be open for the 15th December and at the rate they were working I would have been lucky to get open for the following Valentine's Day. I was rapidly approaching a nervous breakdown at this point but the following ten days gave me some faith in the power of human endeavour. There was no floor in the kitchen, no toilets, no plumbing, no electricity and not a square inch of wall was painted. Things weren't looking good and I had a booking for forty-five people in ten days time. Those ten days were the most stressful of my life. Even twenty-four hours before opening there was nothing painted and no carpet. People were coming in to make deliveries and asking when the restaurant was opening. When I said that it was opening the next day they just laughed out loud. I told them to come back the next day and have a look. Most of them did and just couldn't believe what we had managed to do in such a short space of time.

The new contractors arrived and to say that they

Snapshots taken the day before opening

WHEN I SAID THAT WE WERE
OPENING THE NEXT DAY THEY
JUST LAUGHED OUT LOUD

dinner with juliet

were like angels sent down from the heavens would be doing them an injustice. I have never seen people working so hard. Instead of arguing with all the other tradesmen they were all working together. Finally I could see the place turning into a restaurant and the optimism I had felt on the night I had decided to do this, which had been seeping away, returned with a vengeance.

During all this time that the restaurant was getting fitted out there was so many other things to think about. Most important was the staff. Getting staff is notoriously difficult, particularly in a city like Edinburgh that has very low unemployment. In my experience only one out of every ten people who arrange an interview actually bother to turn up. Eighty percent of the people you actually interview are virtually unemployable. When you ask them the reason for leaving their last job, the answers can range from:

'I had a fight with my last boss and ended up punching him so he told me not to come back.'

'I got the sack for stealing but it wasn't my fault, I've got a gambling addiction.'

Also, in an industry where hygiene is paramount, you would not believe how many chefs turn up for interviews in desperate need of a good bath.

Eventually I did find staff that all managed to prove themselves on their first day at work when they were handed a paintbrush as there was no kitchen to cook in. Here is another dilemma for the budding

restaurateur. What food are you going to cook? I had always told people that the kind of food we would be serving would be 'Modern Scottish' but to be honest with you I'm not exactly sure what constitutes Scottish food alone, never mind the modern variety.

When I think of Scottish food, two-for-the-price-of-one offers at your local frozen food shop spring to mind with everything either deep-fried or boiled. All the food would, of course come with the choice of red or brown sauce. An actual Scottish restaurant would have to have a waitress who only deigned to serve the customers once her phone conversation with her boyfriend Darren was well and truly over. The modern part would come from the whisky and irn-bru cocktail with an olive in it that we would serve as an apéritif.

Although I still classify the restaurant as Scottish, we have ingredients on the menu such as pineapple, mango and coconut which are about as Scottish as a successful national football team. I did decide that I would not have a non-smoking section of the restaurant and that our only smoking policy would be that you have to bring your own fags — very Scottish. I thought that the waiting staff could greet the customers by saying, 'Come on in, you'll have had your tea', though this might not be a good policy for a restaurant and after all we are in Edinburgh and people might take us seriously.

ALTHOUGH I STILL CLASSIFY THE RESTAURANT AS SCOTTISH, WE HAVE INGREDIENTS ON THE MENU SUCH AS PINEAPPLE... WHICH ARE ABOUT AS SCOTTISH AS A SUCCESSFUL NATIONAL FOOTBALL TEAM

One good part of the two, miserable, wilderness years was that I threw lots of dinner parties to test new recipes for the restaurant. I had made my mind up that I did not want the restaurant to be 'trendy'. I wanted it to look luxurious but different. The décor in the restaurant was going to be classical with a modern twist and the food was going to reflect this. At the time the fashion in food was to add a hundred and one flavours to everything to the extent that you weren't sure what you were eating. When I say that the food is Scottish in my restaurant, I mean that we use the best Scottish produce and serve it in a way that compliments the flavour of the main part of the dish. I found my recipes to be a big hit with my dinner party guests. Deciding what food to serve was the easiest part of the process and definitely the most enjoyable.

For our opening night, we were planning to serve warm salads of Parma Ham and Mozzarella, Braised Lamb Shanks and Mulled Winter Fruits, to name but a few dishes. Even at this stage I didn't know if we would make it on time. I phoned the contact for the booking three times to cancel it. Each time the number was engaged so I decided that we would go ahead and take a chance.

The opening night was looming. In the last twenty-four hours the carpet was being laid, chairs and tables were being delivered and miraculously food was being cooked. When the first of the forty-five people turned up I had to send them away to the pub for an hour, as the tables hadn't been set yet. When they came back everything was ready but only just. This was the point where a miracle happened.

I had been preparing for a disaster to happen on my opening night. Every night I had been having nightmares about it. All of the staff was new, the kitchen equipment had only just been fitted and I was physically exhausted. Yet somehow everything went without a hitch. Champagne was served, the food came out perfectly cooked and on time and everybody had a great evening.

When I think back to that night I still don't know how I did it. It has to be said that there were still some things that had to be finished off and smartened up but the restaurant had finally opened and was looking wonderful. My food was going down a storm. The atmosphere was warm, cosy and romantic. Frank Sinatra was coming through the speakers, telling us how young we make him feel. Although I felt that I had aged by ten years in the last twenty-four months I thought that I had finally arrived at the ball and that the culinary world was at my feet. There didn't seem any way that the restaurant could fail to be busy.

I had finished a long hard journey and was finally at my destination. Little did I know that the journey had only just begun and the next stretch of it would have the ups and downs of a roller coaster ride. It wouldn't be long before the glass coach turned back to a pumpkin. There are only two things a girl can do when this happens — let everything fall apart or fight back and make pumpkin soup.

I HAD FINISHED A LONG HARD JOURNEY AND WAS FINALLY AT MY DESTINATION. LITTLE DID I KNOW THAT THE JOURNEY HAD ONLY JUST BEGUN

starters

dinner with juliet

Canapés

We always serve our customers a canapé on arrival, which makes people feel pampered and adds to the luxurious feel of the restaurant.

Clams with Lemon and Ginger Butter

50 g (2 oz) butter
50 g (2 oz) stem ginger
Grated zest of 2 lemons
12 clams, opened by steaming for 1 minute
Black pepper to season

Soften the butter and chop the ginger finely. Beat the butter, ginger and lemon zest together with a wooden spoon and place a teaspoon on each clam. Grill for 2 minutes and season with black pepper.
Serves 4

Duck and Plum Sauce Pancakes

1 duck breast, skin removed
¼ cucumber
3 spring onions
2 plums
½ tbsp soy sauce

Few drops Tabasco sauce
1 tbsp brown sugar
Salt and black pepper to season
4 Chinese pancakes

Cut the duck breast into thin strips and fry until cooked. Cut the cucumber and 2 of the spring onions into 7.5cm / 3 inch long, thin strips. Cut the other spring onion into long thin strips. Stone and slice the plums. Place in a pan with the soy sauce, Tabasco, sugar and a little water to cover. Simmer until the plums are soft and breaking up. Purée the mixture with a hand blender or in a food processor and season to taste. Half the pancakes and place some cucumber, spring onion and duck on each half. Drizzle with the sauce. Fold the pancakes into a cone shape and tie to secure with a long strip of spring onion.
Serves 4

Marinated Olives

275 g (10 oz) olives- black, green or both
Juice and zest of 1 lemon
275 ml (½ pt) olive oil
2 red chillies, finely chopped
Ground black pepper
2 tsp sugar

If the olives are bought in brine, strain and rinse well. Whisk together all of the other ingredients and pour over the olives. Allow to marinate for at least one day and drain off the oil to serve. Keep the oil as it makes a good salad dressing.
Serves 4

dinner with juliet

CARROT, ORANGE AND CORIANDER SOUP WITH BAGEL CROÛTONS

If you can't be bothered to make stock it is perfectly acceptable to add extra orange juice and an extra onion instead. I have always thought that bagels make excellent croûtons, and for this recipe I always use the cinnamon and raisin variety.

2 large onions
550 g (1¼ lb) carrots
2 tbsp olive oil
570 ml (1 pt) chicken or
vegetable stock (see page 182)
570 ml (1 pt) orange juice

3 tbsp freshly chopped
coriander
Salt and pepper to season
150 ml (¼ pt) double cream
2 bagels

Finely chop the onions and carrots, and in a large pot, sweat in half the olive oil until softened but not browned. Add the stock and orange juice and simmer until the carrots are very soft and well cooked. Add the coriander and purée the lot with a hand blender or in a food processor. Season to taste. The cream can either be mixed in or swirled on the top just before the soup is served. To make the croûtons, cut the bagels into thin disks and shallow fry in the remaining olive oil until crispy. Float on top of the soup.
Serves 4

dinner with juliet

Mediterranean Fish Soup

Almost everyone that eats this soup in the restaurant asks for the recipe! There are some dishes that make you feel as if you are on holiday, and this is one of them. The recipe works well as a soup but can be converted into a main course by adding boiled, new potatoes and extra seafood towards the end.

Little vegetable or any cooking oil
1 each red, green and yellow peppers
2 large onions
8 slices unsmoked back bacon
275 ml (½ pt) white wine
570 ml (1 pt) fish stock (see page 183)
2 x 400 g cans chopped tomatoes
4 tbsp tomato purée
1 tbsp sugar
2 tsp balsamic vinegar
2 tbsp sherry
Salt and pepper to season
12 green shell mussels
8 tiger prawns, peeled and deveined
5 sprigs fresh basil
1 clove garlic
150 ml (¼ pt) extra virgin olive oil

Rub a little oil into the peppers, place them on a baking sheet and roast in the oven for 15 minutes or until the skins have begun to blacken. Allow to cool then remove the skins and seeds, and chop finely. Chop the onion finely and cube the bacon. Sweat in a large pot until the onions have softened and the bacon is cooked. Add the white wine and boil until reduced by half. Add the stock, tomatoes, purée and sugar. Allow to simmer for 20 minutes. Add the balsamic vinegar, sherry and season to taste. Add the mussels and prawns and simmer for 5 minutes or until cooked. To make the basil oil, put the basil, garlic and olive oil in a blender and whiz until well incorporated. Drizzle over the soup to serve.

Warning: Basil oil should be used immediately and any remaining oil should be disposed of.
Serves 4

SALAD OF HOME-CURED SALMON

Although this recipe does not involve any cooking the results are very tasty and will make you think twice about buying smoked salmon. Once made, the salmon can be used in pasta dishes and salads but is especially nice in a sandwich with cucumber and mayonnaise. Wild salmon will give better results but the farmed variety will do.

225 g (8 oz) fresh salmon
5 tbsp sea salt
150 ml (¼ pt) olive oil
Juice and finely grated rind of 2 lemons
2 tbsp chopped dill
1 tbsp sugar

3 tbsp sherry
Ground black pepper
Crispy salad leaves
Scottish oatcakes (see page 183)
Little mayonnaise (see page 183)

Place the salmon in a bowl and cover well with the sea salt. Cover the bowl with cling film and refrigerate overnight. The next day, rinse the salmon; it should feel a little bit hard and leathery. Place in a clean bowl. To make the marinade, whisk together the olive oil, lemon juice and rind, dill, sugar, sherry and pepper. Pour over the salmon and leave covered in the fridge overnight. Carve the salmon finely and serve with the salad leaves, oatcakes and mayonnaise.

Serves 4

MUSSELS IN CREAM, WHITE WINE AND SAFFRON

I have tried many different kinds of wine for this recipe but I think that unoaked Chardonnay works best. This dish is best served with hot, crusty bread to mop up the sauce. Some spaghetti tossed through the mussels and sauce converts this recipe into a tasty supper dish.

4 shallots, finely chopped
Little olive oil
450 ml (¾ pt) white wine (preferably unoaked Chardonnay)
Pinch of Saffron
900 g (2 lb) mussels, cleaned and scrubbed with the beards removed
450 ml (¾ pt) double cream
Pinch sugar
Ground black pepper
1 spring onion, finely chopped

In a large pot that has a lid, sweat the shallots in the olive oil. Add the white wine and the saffron and bring to the boil. Add the mussels and cover the pot with the lid, allowing the wine to continue simmering. Cook for 5 minutes or until the mussels have opened, shaking the pot at intervals. Remove the mussels from the wine, discarding any that have not opened. Bring the wine to the boil and reduce by half. Add the cream and allow to boil until the sauce has reduced by one-third and is thick enough to coat the back of a spoon. Add the sugar and black pepper to taste. Divide into deep bowls and garnish with the spring onion.
Serves 4

TWICE-BAKED CHEESE AND WATERCRESS SOUFFLÉS

This is a dream dinner party starter as soufflés are always impressive, and this one can be made in advance. The choice of cheese is pretty much up to you but I like to use, either all blue cheese, or a mixture of cheddar, mozzarella and a little Parmesan.

50 g (2 oz) butter
25 g (1 oz) flour
450 ml (¾ pt) milk
5 egg yolks
150 g (5 oz) cheese
Handful watercress
Salt and black pepper to season
6 egg whites
275 ml (½ pt) double cream

In a saucepan, melt the butter. Add the flour and mix well. Pour over the milk and whisk until well mixed. Leave on the heat, stirring all the time until the sauce has thickened and coats the back of a spoon easily. Set aside one-third of the sauce. Add the egg yolks to the rest, whisking all the time. Add the cheese (reserving 2 tablespoons for sprinkling at the end) and half of the watercress. Season to taste.

Whisk the egg whites until they form stiff peaks. Using a large metal spoon fold one-third of the egg whites into the sauce and then fold in the rest. Spoon the mixture into greased individual ramekins. Place in an ovenproof dish and pour water in the dish so that it comes half way up the ramekins. Bake at 180°C / 350°F / gas mark 4 for 15 to 20 minutes or until golden and well risen; leave to cool. The soufflés will shrink and flop in the middle, but don't worry, they will rise again on their second baking. Run a sharp knife round the edges of the soufflés and turn out.

Add the cream and the remaining watercress to the sauce that was set aside and purée with a hand blender or in a food processor. Everything can be made up to this stage in advance. To finish, place the soufflés on individual ovenproof dishes. Pour over the sauce and sprinkle with the remaining cheese. Bake at 220°C / 425°F / gas mark 7 for 6 to 8 minutes until re-risen and golden on top. Serve immediately.
Serves 4

Tiger Prawns and Scallops in a Papaya and Lime Sauce

Papaya and lime go together brilliantly, and you will be surprised at how well fruit works with seafood. Be sure to ask your fishmonger for some scallop shells to serve the seafood in.

2 papaya
Juice and finely grated rind of 2 limes
50 g (2 oz) butter
Salt and black pepper to season
12 raw large tiger prawns, shelled and deveined
12 king scallops

Halve the papaya and scoop out the seeds. Scoop out the fruit and chop finely. Cook the papaya in a pan, over a low heat, with the lime juice and zest. Whisk in the butter and season to taste. Add the prawns and scallops and cook, stirring all the time until they are firm to the touch. Serve in the scallop shells or the hollow shells of the papaya.
Serves 4

Risotto Fritters with Fiery Salsa

It may seem strange to make risotto into balls and then deep-fry them. This dish, however, is a lovely little starter that can be prepared in advance and deep-fried at the last minute. The hot salsa offsets the creamy risotto well.

For the risotto fritters:
1 onion
1 tbsp olive oil
125 g (4 oz) Arborio rice
50 g (2 oz) sun-dried tomatoes
600 ml (1 pt) chicken or vegetable stock (page 182)

150 ml (¼ pt) double cream
3 basil leaves, coarsely chopped
Salt and black pepper to season
2 buffalo mozzarella cheese
2 eggs, beaten
75 g (3 oz) breadcrumbs

Finely chop the onion and sweat in a pan with the olive oil. Add the rice and cook for about 2 minutes until each grain is well-coated in oil. Add the sun-dried tomatoes and stir.

In a separate pot bring the stock to simmering point. Add the stock to the rice gradually, ladling more in as each lot is absorbed. Repeat until the rice is cooked. Add the double cream and basil. Season to taste. Transfer the mixture into a shallow container and chill. Once chilled, the risotto should be quite firm and pliable. Cut the mozzarella into 2.5cm / 1 inch cubes, and mould some of the risotto round each cube to form small balls. Roll the balls in the egg then the breadcrumbs twice over. Deep fry the balls in hot oil until they are golden brown. When cut apart the mozzarella should be melted in the middle.

For the salsa:
150 g (5 oz) cherry tomatoes
1 each red, green and yellow peppers
6 stems fresh coriander
2 red chillies

2 green chillies
2 tbsp lime juice
2 tbsp olive oil
1 tbsp sugar
Salt and black pepper to season

Chop the tomatoes, peppers, coriander and chillies finely. Remember to wash your hands thoroughly after chopping chillies — if you are male you might get something of a shock when you go to the toilet if you don't! In a bowl, whisk the lime juice, oil and sugar. Add the chopped ingredients and season to taste.
Serves 4

GAME TERRINE WITH ONION MARMALADE

People tend to think that terrines are fiddly and difficult. If you ask your game dealer to mince your game meat for you, this will save a lot of time. The sweet onion marmalade is the perfect accompaniment to the strong game and is also delicious served as an accompaniment to a cheese board.

FOR THE TERRINE:
225 g (8 oz) unsmoked back bacon
450 g (1 lb) mixed game meat, minced
110 g (4 oz) chicken liver
110 g (4 oz) dried apricots, coarsely chopped
2 eggs
3 tbsp brandy
Salt and black pepper to season

Line a loaf tin with tinfoil. Stretch the strips of bacon and use most of them to line the tin, overlapping slightly and allowing the ends to hang over the edge of the tin.

Liquidise the liver, apricots, eggs and brandy. In a large bowl mix the game meat and liver mixture. Add a little salt and pepper to season. Fry a little of the game mix to check the seasoning and adjust accordingly. Put the mix into the bacon-lined tin, pushing into the edges. Put a couple of strips of bacon along the top of the terrine and bring round the overlapping bacon.

Cover with tinfoil and place the tin in a larger ovenproof dish. Carefully pour water into the ovenproof dish until it is half way up the tin. Bake at 170°C / 325°F / gas mark 3 for 45 minutes to 1 hour or until a sharp knife inserted into the terrine comes out hot and the juices run clear. Allow to cool in the tin, then turn out and carve into slices with a sharp knife.

FOR THE ONION MARMALADE:
2 red onions
275 ml (½ pt) orange juice
4 tbsp brown sugar

Slice the onions finely. Put in a saucepan over a medium heat with the orange juice and sugar. Allow to simmer and reduce, stirring occasionally until thick and sticky. This will take approximately 15 minutes to thicken.
Serves 4

STEAK TARTARE

Every chef has their own version of this. Call me biased but I think mine is the best! You must use a piece of super lean, well-hung fillet steak. Making this dish a few hours in advance has its benefits, as the flavours will develop. I like to eat this with Melba toast, some crunchy salad and home-made mayonnaise. (See pages 187 and 183 for Melba toast and Mayonnaise recipes.)

350 g (12 oz) fillet steak
2 shallots
1 tbsp capers
1 egg yolk
1 tsp Tabasco sauce
2 tsp tomato ketchup
Salt and black pepper to season

Put all the ingredients in a food processor and pulse until finely chopped but still rough. Alternatively chop the steak, shallots and caper by hand then mix in the other ingredients. Adjust the seasoning and add more Tabasco if you like things spicy.
Serves 4

dinner with juliet

Parma ham, Mozzarella and Fig salad with Balsamic Dressing

This is one of my favourites – the ingredients used could have been made for each other. Knowing how to make a good balsamic dressing will serve you well, as it always makes a salad seem quite decadent and, therefore, a diet slightly less harrowing.

8 slices Parma ham
4 figs
2 baby mozzarella
Salad leaves

For the balsamic dressing:
1 tbsp balsamic vinegar
1 tbsp red wine vinegar
3 tbsp olive oil
2 tsp Dijon Mustard
1 tbsp brown sugar
Salt and black pepper to season

Cut the Parma ham into thin strips. Quarter the figs and mozzarella. Wrap each piece of fig and mozzarella in Parma ham. Place on a baking sheet and grill for 2 minutes until the Parma ham begins to go crispy and the mozzarella softens.

Meanwhile, whisk all the ingredients for the dressing together until well blended and the sugar has dissolved. Season to taste. Serve the mozzarella and fig rolls on a bed of leaves and drizzle over the balsamic dressing.
Serves 4

dinner with juliet

WARM SALAD OF DUCK WITH SESAME AND GINGER

Preserved stem ginger is one of my favourite ingredients and is very tasty combined with the sesame flavour. The duck can be replaced with an equivalent amount of chicken, beef or even pigeon breast.

2 fillets of Barbary or Gressingham duck
2 tbsp vegetable oil
1 tbsp sesame seeds
3 pieces stem ginger, finely chopped plus 2 tbsp of syrup from the jar
1 tbsp sesame oil
1 tbsp lime juice
Salt and black pepper to season
2 plums, stoned and sliced
Salad leaves

With a sharp knife, make slashes in the duck skin 3 mm / ⅛ inch apart. Heat 1 tablespoon of the vegetable oil in a frying pan, then fry the duck breasts for 3 minutes or until the skin is crispy and a lot of the fat has been rendered. Pour off the fat and discard or save for making roast potatoes. Turn the duck breasts and fry for a further 3 minutes until the other side is well browned. Remove from the pan and slice thinly. Add the sesame seeds to the pan and allow to brown slightly. Add the stem ginger and syrup, sesame oil, the remaining vegetable oil and lime juice. Whisk well and season to taste. Add the duck and plums to the dressing and heat through. Toss the warm ingredients with the salad leaves.
Serves 4

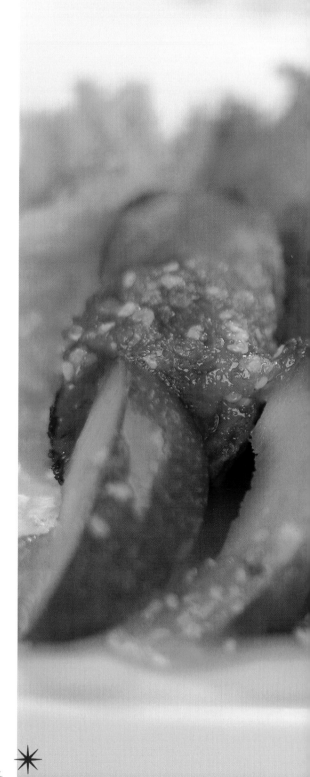

WARM SALAD OF VENISON AND BERRIES

Venison works very well with fruity flavours. Finding a good game dealer is invaluable. I use George Bowers in Stockbridge. You could use frozen berries for this recipe if you can't get fresh. I like to eat this dish with a glass of chilled, sparkling Merlot. Although fizzy red wine is not to everyone's taste, it is light enough to drink with a salad but takes on the more heady flavours well.

275 g (10 oz) venison fillet
2 tbsp olive oil
150 g (5 oz) mixed berries
2 tbsp red wine vinegar
Salt and black pepper to season
Watercress and lambs lettuce leaves

Cut the venison into thin strips and fry on each side in 1 tablespoon of the olive oil for 2 minutes until cooked. Remove from the pan and add half of the berries and the vinegar. Stir over a low heat until the berries are soft and falling apart. Whisk to break up the berries and whisk in the remaining olive oil. Season to taste. Return the venison to the pan and warm through. Arrange on the salad leaves with the remaining berries.
Serves 4

STOCKBRIDGE RESTAURANT CHICKEN SALAD

This salad has a fun, exotic appearance, and I like to think that it tastes of summer. It is worthwhile going for a good quality piece of free-range chicken as most chickens these days are lacking flavour. This is a lovely dish to prepare for a picnic.

2 chicken breasts, skin removed
2 tbsp lemon juice
2 tbsp sherry
2 small pineapples
110 g (4 oz) strawberries
2 tbsp mayonnaise
3 tbsp lime juice
2 tsp sugar
2 tbsp freshly chopped coriander
Salt and black pepper to season
Few crispy salad leaves

Slice the chicken breasts thinly, and in a shallow dish cover with the lemon juice and sherry. Cover and refrigerate for 2 hours. Remove the chicken from the marinade and pat dry. Fry or grill the chicken until cooked. Cut the pineapples in half and with a sharp knife remove the fruit so that you are left with four hollow halves. Chop the pineapple fruit into cubes and hull and half the strawberries. Whisk together the mayonnaise, lime juice, sugar and coriander. Season to taste. Arrange the leaves, chicken, strawberries and pineapple in the pineapple halves and drizzle with the dressing.
Serves 4

SORBETS

This is another little touch that makes the restaurant so special. We serve these sorbets in little shot glasses between the starters and main courses as a palate cleanser. If you don't have an ice cream maker, don't worry; just let the mix go solid and then mash it up with a fork. These recipes are designed to be refreshing so will be more icy and not as sweet as traditional sorbets.

BERRY AND COINTREAU

225 g (8 oz) mixed berries
2 tbsp sugar
2 tbsp lemon juice
2 tbsp Cointreau

Put all the ingredients into a blender and whiz until well puréed. Churn until frozen in an ice cream maker or freeze in a Tupperware container until nearly solid then mash with a fork.

VODKA AND CITRUS

150 ml (¼ pt) orange juice
2 tbsp lemon juice
1 tbsp lime juice
3 tbsp sugar
2 tbsp vodka

Put all the ingredients into a pan and stir over a low heat until the sugar is dissolved. Churn until frozen or freeze until nearly solid then mash with a fork.

APPLE AND CALVADOS

225 g (8 oz) Brambly apples
3 tbsp sugar
2 tbsp Calvados

Peel, quarter and core the apples and cook in a saucepan with the sugar until very soft. Add the Calvados and purée with a hand blender or in a food processor until smooth. Churn until frozen or freeze until nearly solid then mash with a fork.
Serves 4

Making

dreams come true

NOBODY GETS AS EXCITED AS ME UPON DISCOVERING A NEW INGREDIENT OR CREATING A DIFFERENT RECIPE.

dinner with juliet

MAKING DREAMS
COME TRUE

After my successful opening night, things went rapidly downhill and pumpkin soup was being made left, right and centre. The trouble was that nobody was coming in to eat the stuff. Christmas came and went, and the only Christmas spirit I enjoyed was the one that comes in a bottle. New year was no different. With the changing digits of the calendar comes a new hope and optimism but for me it only lasted until the last glass of champagne wore off.

For over two years I had focused on the opening night of my restaurant and when your opening night is fully booked, that's a lot to look forward to. I never thought for one moment that there was a chance that I wouldn't be successful. Having an entrepreneurial spirit comes with risks and I was aware that it was going to be a struggle but not to the extent that it was. To be honest, I didn't think so much about what work would be like after that first busy night.

I have read countless interviews with well-known chefs who are quite prepared to harp on about how the main ingredient for running a successful restaurant is passion for food. Now I am as passionate about cooking as the next chef, probably even more so. I have more passion for cooking than I had for any of my ex-boyfriends but if you met some of them you might see why. Nobody gets as excited as me upon discovering a new ingredient or creating a different recipe. I had

passion. I had a beautiful restaurant and fantastic food to serve too but none of these things were making me successful.

Instead of waiting tables the staff were waiting to leave with a bit of light glass polishing thrown in. There were times when I thought that they would wear holes in those glasses. During the quiet times there is only so much cleaning your staff can do. Keeping them occupied is a full-time operation. It's when they start making drawings of each other and doing crosswords that you want to weep.

Running a busy restaurant is far easier than running a quiet one. If you are constantly busy you know how many staff you need, what food to order and most importantly, you can predict how much income your business is going to generate. The ironic thing is that it is much more tiring running a quiet business than a busy one. After a busy night I often feel as if I could do the whole evening again. Being a chef is a very physical job but the energy comes from the adrenalin buzz that comes from knowing that people want to eat your food. The worry of your business being quiet is simply exhausting. Although you are surrounded by food, the prospect of chewing your own head off seems like a better option than eating it.

If you have ever wondered why so many restaurateurs become alcoholics, the answer is simple. When you finish work there is no way you can go home and straight to bed. You have to wind down first. I usually watch some rubbish on the television for an hour. Late night telly is completely dire and there's not as much porn on channel five as everyone seems to think, mores the pity. When you finish work and its so late that there's nothing to do — not forgetting the fact that everyone else is in bed — its quite easy to drink too much, especially when you have a cellar full of wine. Stopping your wine cellar from becoming

RUNNING A BUSY RESTAURANT IS FAR EASIER THAN RUNNING A QUIET ONE

your best friend is the hard part. I have been known to sit in there and have a cry once or twice when things became too much. Luckily I didn't make the mistake of taking a corkscrew in with me.

Sometimes I can't believe that I managed to get through my first year of business without developing a drink problem. The nervous tick is under control now but can still reappear when somebody mentions the word, 'OVERDRAFT'.

Here is the rub: when the cash isn't coming in it still has to go out. What do you do if the bills are mounting up and your overdraft is at its limit? It wasn't just current expenditure either. I was still paying start-up costs too. When I was in that situation a lot of pride had to be swallowed. I became an expert at juggling my finances, not an easy task when you've got no finances to speak of. I just had to tell people that I would pay them so much now and the rest later. Sprinting up to the post office to pay the phone bill at the last minute may be good exercise but not much fun.

I seriously considered selling my flat at one point and getting a smaller, cheaper one so I could put some money in the coffers but I couldn't get another mortgage because I am now self-employed. My full time staff can get a mortgage, of course, which I would

give them a reference for but financial institutions don't seem to realise that if there were redundancies going the boss would be the last to go. Personal loans, business loans and an extension of my overdraft were all refused. I recently found out that I might have been given an extension on my overdraft but my bank manager didn't realise that I had signed a personal guarantee to cover any finance that they lent me — that's service for you.

I know that a lot of people think that money isn't important and that's fair enough but the type of person who thinks that way probably isn't super rich but has always had a regular income. I was in the kind of situation where money was the most important thing in the world. Throughout this time I didn't even buy a lottery ticket, as I wanted any financial rewards to come from the success of the restaurant.

It wasn't only my bank account that was dented but my pride too. I was only twenty-five years old when the restaurant opened and there were plenty of people who doubted my ability to run it and would have been quite happy to see me fall flat on my face. This image is still easily accessible if you manage to catch me out on one Pinot Grigio too many, standing on heels one inch too high.

It may sound pathetic but I was more often than not on the verge of tears with the worry of it all. There

AT ONE POINT I CONSIDERED TURNING THE RESTAURANT INTO A CAFÉ-BAR, ANYTHING TO MAKE THE PLACE BUSIER

were times that opening the door to the restaurant felt like stepping into my own personal room 101. At one point I considered turning the restaurant into a café-bar, anything to make the place busier. I could have sold the lease and at least got some of my investment back but what would that mean? — Failure. Not an option. I wasn't going to give up yet.

Yet I was still more depressed than Leonard Cohen on a bad day. The key to the success of a restaurant is customers — and plenty of them. There are three things that help you get your customers when you finally open your doors and here they are — location, location and location. If you open up in the right location and serve utter rubbish you can have a busy restaurant. Throw in some rude staff and uncomfortable chairs and you can have a chain of

CUSTOMERS WERE FINALLY COMING IN AND WHAT A WELCOME SIGHT THEY WERE

successful restaurants. I may sound very bitter but there was at least a passion in my bitterness.

Stockbridge is the sort of place that was once a very bohemian area and in many respects still is. There are wine barfuls of young professional couples moving in and out of the area and making a killing in their house sales. I thought that I had found the perfect location for an upmarket, luxurious restaurant. I didn't want to have the kind of place where customers were under pressure to finish their desserts because someone was waiting for their table. I wanted people to enjoy the whole experience of an evening out, not just a meal. Eventually, after a great deal of patience, things started to pay off. Bookings were in the diary. Customers were finally coming in and what a welcome sight they were.

I would say that about ninety percent of my customers are lovely decent people but you do get the odd one or two that can be either rude or candidates for a straightjacket and padded cell. The first night that we were full since we opened was the following Valentine's Day. Personally I'm not too keen on this day of the year as I think that it was invented by a sixteenth-century greetings card manufacturer as a way of torturing young women, when they weren't burning them at the stake for practicing witchcraft. However, it still remains one of the most important dates in the restaurateurs' diary as you could fill you restaurant five times over on Valentine's Day.

If you have the misfortune of being single on this dreaded day and spend hours envying the couples that book up every restaurant in town, think again. Most of the couples have fallen out before they get to the restaurant. This is usually because the husband or boyfriend has failed to buy an appropriate present. When we handed the ladies a complimentary rose, the withering — more than you damn well bothered to do — look they gave their other half sent such a chill through the dining room we had to turn the heating up. They were such a romantic lot that we didn't sell one bottle of champagne and one couple even stole the salt and pepper grinders (presumably as a last minute gift). Needless to say there were no proposals that evening, though one woman was so livid with her partner it wouldn't have surprised me if there had been a murder.

We have had two proposals in the restaurant. The first time this happened was during a busy Saturday night. The bloke gingerly got down on one knee, popped the question and the young lady was so delighted she practically had to be restrained from doing a tap dance round the dining room. The whole thing certainly had the 'Ah' factor and a round of applause ensued. Unfortunately the rampant

WE HAVE HAD
TWO PROPOSALS IN
THE RESTAURANT

snogging that followed the slipping on of the ring was enough to put some people off their crème brûlée.

We didn't even know that the second proposal was happening until the woman had stalked out of the restaurant and a distraught man was left sitting on his own. Things were winding down by this time so some of the waitresses decided to have a drink with Mr Reject and cheer him up — there's nothing girls love more than a pitiful man who looks like an orphaned puppy. This sad tale does, however, have a happy ending as one of the waitresses is now dating Mr Reject-No-Longer.

We have had a few famous people dine in the restaurant and as always, they look smaller than they do on the telly. There was one time that a blonde, female television presenter came in when we were completely full, demanding a table for two immediately. When the waitress told her we were full, she kicked up such a stink and I had to come out of the kitchen to deal with her. I tried to explain that every table was taken and there was no way we could accommodate her. Then came the most pathetic sentence ever: 'Do you know who I am?' I had to stop myself from replying, 'Yes I do, you're the old slapper on the telly.' Instead I gave an answer that was brutally honest: 'Madam if you have to ask me that question then I either don't know or don't care.' So she stropped out, slamming the door behind her. I can

only presume that she wanted me to throw some customers out in the middle of their meal to accommodate her.

Every restaurant occasionally gets a table of people that have decided to come out for the evening and have a horrible time. Not only are they determined not to enjoy themselves but are quite adamant in their quest to make sure that the staff's lives are made utterly miserable too. On one such evening we had a table of four who seemed to be determined to make the Spanish waitress cry. Every time the poor girl came into the kitchen they had said a horrible thing about Spain or done something nasty to her like moving the wine glass as she was pouring the wine. I am very protective of my waiting staff as it's a hard job and they really try to make people have a good time. Most of them are students, so waiting tables isn't a vocation for them but they make the best of it and I am proud to say that they enjoy working in the restaurant. On this occasion the poor Spanish waitress was not enjoying her job at all.

It got to the stage that I saw red and had to take drastic action. Luckily I happened to have a glove puppet in my handbag, which I had recently kidnapped from my ex-boyfriends flat (honestly I'm not making this up). The glove puppet was called 'Donkey', as it was a donkey and it is incredibly cute. I don't know what possessed me to do this but it was one of the brightest ideas I have ever had.

I put the glove puppet on my hand and went up to the nasty table. 'Donkey would like to say hello to you' Donkey's little arm was waving, 'Hello Donkey!' They were waving back. I made donkey whisper in my ear (I really am quite accomplished in puppetry skills, you know), 'Donkey would like to know if you are having a nice time?' Donkey looked at them expectantly and they replied in unison, 'Yes Donkey we are.'

Donkey said his goodbyes but the funny thing was that the table never mentioned to each other what had happened. It was as if they had made some kind of silent pact to keep it to themselves. The lesson of this story, however is that they were as nice as could be after their meeting with Donkey and you would have thought that the waitress was their daughter.

Since that night I have used Donkey several times to diffuse an awkward situation. I would advise anyone who works with the public to buy themselves a glove puppet as it makes life so much easier. Donkey has proved to be such an effective member of staff that I am thinking of making him a director of the company.

By far my favourite customers are the large parties. This is for several reasons. Firstly, they bring a good atmosphere to the restaurant as they are usually

I'M REALLY SURPRISED
THAT THE NEIGHBOURS
DON'T COMPLAIN ABOUT
THE BAD SINGING AT THIS TIME
OF YEAR AS IT FELT AS IF THE
'HAPPY BIRTHDAY' SONG WAS
SUNG EVERY NIGHT.

SO WAS ALL THE STRUGGLING AND WORRY WORTH IT? I CAN HONESTLY SAY THAT IT WAS

livelier and this rubs off on the tables of two making the mood in the restaurant a bit more partyish. Secondly it is a damn sight easier serving and cooking for a table of ten rather than five tables of two and also big tables tend to drink lots of wine and consequently spend more money.

Often the big tables tend to be birthday parties. There must be nothing worth watching on the telly in March because everybody seems to have their birthday in January. I'm really surprised that the neighbours don't complain about the bad singing at this time of year as it felt as if the 'Happy Birthday' song was sung every night.

I was brought up with the philosophy that if you are going to do something, make a decent job of it or don't bother. When it comes to singing 'Happy Birthday' my staff have not always shared this view. I

nearly lost it with them one evening when, for the umpteenth time, I trotted out of the kitchen with the birthday cake, belting out the dreaded song (my singing voice can make cat-wailing sound like Pavarotti) while they stood behind me mouthing the words. In the end they were told in no uncertain terms that they looked like a bigger bunch of fools being sheepish about the whole thing than if they made a show of it. Thankfully we now have a chorus of singers that could rival a small village operatic society.

So was all the struggling and worry worth it? I can honestly say that it was. Turning people away because you are full, having people tell you what a great time and good food they have had, becoming known for being a top restaurant and not to mention being able to pay your bills — all these things make it worthwhile.

The financial rewards are still a long time coming but the feeling I have when I think back to the hard times and how I got through them with my sanity almost intact, the pride I can feel in myself, is one of the biggest rewards I could get. I am now so proud of telling people which restaurant I own. Needless to say they are often surprised that someone of my age has such a lovely, successful place. Feeding a restaurant full of people who have all come to taste my cooking is the best feeling in the world and not a spoonful of pumpkin soup in sight.

main courses

seafood

dinner with juliet

Gratin of Tiger Prawns and Monkfish with Coconut and Mango

This recipe has been on our menu from day one and is extremely popular. If you can't get hold of fresh ripe mangoes, the tinned variety works well – or you could use pineapple instead.

16 large raw tiger prawns, shelled and deveined
350 g (12 oz) monkfish, cut into 16 pieces
Block creamed coconut
3 mangoes, peeled and cubed
150 ml (¼ pt) double cream
Ground black pepper

Either divide the prawns and monkfish amongst four gratin dishes or spread out in one big dish. Cut the coconut block into small pieces and dissolve in a pan with 150 ml (¼ pt) of water, over a gentle heat. Add two-thirds of the mango and heat until well softened. Add the cream and black pepper to taste. Purée the sauce using a hand blender or in a food processor. Place the remaining mango in the dish(es) and pour over the sauce. Bake at 200°C / 400°F / gas mark 6 for 15 minutes or until the fish is firm to the touch.
Serves 4

Fillet of Sea Bass in a Soufflé Sauce

This recipe works well because you get a crispy soufflé on the top but a creamy sauce underneath. Although I have used almonds and grapes in this recipe, you could substitute them for Parma ham or lightly sautéed leeks, which also work well.

1 small onion, finely chopped
Little vegetable oil or any cooking oil
275 ml (½ pt) dry white wine
450 ml (¾ pt) double cream
Salt and black pepper to season
4 fillets of sea bass, skinned
225 g (8 oz) seedless green grapes, halved
3 tbsp flaked almonds
3 egg yolks
6 egg whites

Lightly fry the onion in the oil until golden. Add the white wine and bring to the boil. Reduce by half. Add the cream and reduce until the sauce coats the back of a spoon. Season to taste. Divide the fish fillets into four small gratin dishes or place in one big one. Place the grapes and almonds on top of the fish and season. Drizzle half the sauce over the fish. Whisk the egg yolks into the remaining sauce. In a clean bowl, whisk the egg whites until stiff. Using a large metal spoon, fold half of the egg whites into the sauce, and then, gently fold in the rest. Spoon the soufflé mix over the fish and bake at 200°C / 400°F / gas mark 6 for 15 to 20 minutes or until risen and golden and a knife inserted into the fish comes out hot.
Serves 4

LOBSTER IN A CHAMPAGNE SAUCE

This is a lottery winner's meal, if ever I saw one. The debate continues as to the best way to put the poor wee lobsters out of their misery when cooking them. I get them straight from the fridge into the boiling water, as this seems to be the least traumatic. Contrary to popular belief, lobsters do not scream when they are being boiled. Firstly, they have no vocal cords, and secondly, the shock alone kills them instantly. If you think that champagne is too expensive use a good Cava or dry white wine instead.

2 large lobsters, uncooked
75 g (3 oz) butter
2 shallots, finely chopped
450 ml (¾ pt) champagne
450 ml (¾ pt) double cream
2 egg yolks
Salt and black pepper to season

Bring a large pan of water to the boil and put the lobsters in. Simmer for 2 minutes. Remove and cut the lobsters in half. Remove the stomach sack, the intestine and the green roe. Melt the butter in a large pan and add the shallots. Place the lobster, flesh-side down in the pan. Cover and cook over a low heat for 2 minutes. Add the champagne and simmer until reduced by half. Remove the lobster from the pan and add two-thirds of the cream. Simmer for 5 minutes. Whisk the remaining cream and the egg yolks. Remove the meat from the tail of the lobster and cut into slices. Crack and remove the meat from the claw and place all the lobster meat in the shell tails. Take the sauce off the heat and whisk in the cream and egg yolk liaison. Heat gently until thickened but do not allow to boil. Season to taste and pour over the lobster. Place the lobsters under a very hot grill for 1 minute.
Serves 4

Seafood Platter with Sherry Mayonnaise

Sometimes the most simple dishes are the best. I would save this one for summer when the best variety of seafood is in season. I eat this with crispy salad and chips to dip in the sherry mayonnaise.

2 small live lobsters
8 raw jumbo prawns
8 crab claws
25 g (1 oz) butter
8 large king scallops in the half shell
8 oysters

Bring a large pot of water to the boil. Put the lobsters in and poach for 5 minutes. Add the prawns and poach for a further 3 minutes. Add the crab claws and poach for a further 1 minute. Remove all the shellfish and allow to cool. Melt the butter in a frying pan and lightly sauté the scallops for 1 minute on each side or until just firm. Put the scallops back in their shells. Cut the lobsters in half and remove the stomach bag and intestines. Place all the seafood on a bed of crushed ice mixed with rock salt and serve with claw crackers, finger bowls and bibs!

For the mayonnaise:
1 quantity mayonnaise (see page 183)
1 tbsp freshly chopped parsley
1 tbsp freshly chopped chives
2 tbsp dry sherry

Mix the mayonnaise with the parsley and the chives. Stir in the dry sherry then serve with the seafood platter.
Serves 4

SALMON FILLET WITH A CARAMEL SAUCE AND SHERRY BRAISED FENNEL

It might seem odd to eat fish with such a sweet sauce, but salmon takes it on well. Don't be frightened of the strong aniseed aroma of fennel. Much of this is eliminated in the cooking and you are left with quite a delicate flavour.

FOR THE SHERRY BRAISED FENNEL:
2 large fennel bulbs, cut into eighths.
150 ml (¼ pt) dry sherry
2 tbsp olive oil
Salt and black pepper to season

Place the fennel in an ovenproof dish and pour over the sherry and drizzle with the oil. Season and cover with tinfoil. Bake at 200°C / 400°F / gas mark 6 for 20 minutes or until well softened.

FOR THE SALMON AND CARAMEL SAUCE:
4 x 175 g (6 oz) salmon fillets
150 ml (¼ pt) dry white wine
2 tbsp sugar
50 g (2 oz) butter
Salt and black pepper to season

Grill the salmon skin-side up for 10 to 12 minutes or until cooked. Meanwhile, simmer the white wine and sugar, and reduce until thin and syrupy. Whisk in the butter and season to taste. Pour the caramel sauce over the salmon and serve with the braised fennel.
Serves 4

dinner with juliet

PAELLA AND SANGRIA

This is one of my favourite dishes to make and is a lot of fun for a lively dinner party —
especially with lots of sangria to wash it down. It may seem odd putting a cocktail recipe in a
seafood section but the combination is so perfect you won't want one without the other.

SEAFOOD PAELLA

4 tbsp olive oil

450 g–700g (1–1½ lb) seafood (raw
tiger prawns, squid, scallops and
monkfish are best)

20 fresh mussels in their shells, cleaned
and scrubbed

1 onion, finely chopped

225 g (8 oz) chorizo sausage

1 clove of garlic, finely chopped

1 red pepper, chopped

225 g (8 oz) Arborio or paella rice

2 tomatoes, chopped

900 ml (1½ pt) fish stock (see page 183)

150 ml (¼ pt) white wine

Pinch of saffron

Salt and black pepper to season

Lemon wedges, sliced tomato and sliced
peppers to garnish

Heat 2 tablespoons of the olive oil in a large frying pan and stir fry all of the seafood, except
for the mussels, for 2 minutes. Set the lot aside in a bowl with all the juices.

In the same pan heat the rest of the oil and fry the onions, sausage, garlic and red pepper until
the onions have softened. Add the rice and fry for 2 minutes, coating the grains with the oil,
stirring all the time. Add the tomatoes, stock, wine, seafood, mussels and saffron. Season with
the salt and pepper and mix well. Cover the pan and cook over a low, simmering heat for 25 to
30 minutes (check after 20 minutes, and add a little water if the rice is dry) or until the rice is
cooked. Make sure to throw out any mussels that have not opened. Garnish with the lemon,
tomato and peppers.

SANGRIA

Makes 2 pints

Orange slices

Lemon slices

Fruit mixture, such as apples, peaches
and strawberries

Lots of ice

Measure each of brandy, Cointreau,
vodka, grenadine and white rum

570 ml (1 pt) red wine

275 ml (½ pt) lemonade

In a large jug place some of the orange and lemon slices along with any fruit you fancy. Add
plenty of ice and pour over the brandy, Cointreau, vodka, grenadine and white rum. Add the
red wine and the lemonade. Stir well and enjoy.

Serves 4

dinner with juliet

Monkfish, Parma Ham and Mozzarella Parcels with White Wine Braised Asparagus

This is a combination that adds up to a sum of more than its parts. Ask your fishmonger for nice plump pieces of monkfish. It wasn't long ago that you couldn't give monkfish away but now it is super-popular and quite expensive. If you have ever seen a whole one you will know that they aren't the prettiest of creatures, so any semi-vegetarians who eat fish need not feel too guilty.

4 pieces monkfish tail weighing approximately 200 g (7 oz)
4 balls of buffalo mozzarella
12 slices Parma ham
8 spears asparagus
150 ml (¼ pt) white wine
25 g/1 oz butter
Salt and black pepper to season

With a sharp knife cut a slit down the length of the monkfish tails. Stuff the mozzarella into the space then wrap the Parma ham round the fish. Lay on a baking tray. Place the asparagus on a length of tinfoil and bring up the sides of the foil so that the wine can be poured in without spillage. Pour in the wine and add pieces of the butter. Season with salt and pepper and close the foil over the asparagus. If the asparagus is placed at the top of a hot oven (220°C / 425°F / gas mark 7) and the monkfish in the middle they should take 15 to 20 minutes to cook. Carve each portion of monkfish into 4 pieces and arrange on the plates with the asparagus.
Serves 4

POSH FISH AND CHIPS WITH A SUMMER PEA SALAD AND HOME-MADE TOMATO AND TARTAR SAUCE

You have no idea how excited some of our customers are when they see 'fish and chips' on our menu. If you are having a dinner party it is a nice idea to serve this dish wrapped in gold paper or the pages of a glossy magazine for a truly up-market fish supper.

1.1 kg (2½ lb) potatoes
oil for deep frying
4 whole Dover sole, skinned
4 tbsp plain flour

Salt and black pepper to season
50 g (2 oz) butter
2 tbsp vegetable oil

Peel and cut the potatoes into long, thin chips. Heat the oil in a deep-fat frier or a heavy-based saucepan, until a cube of bread tossed in sizzles. Fry the chips until they are soft but have not yet turned golden. Remove from the pan and drain on kitchen paper. Set aside. Dust the fish so that each one is covered with a thin layer of flour. Season each side. Melt the butter with the oil in a pan and fry the sole on each side until just cooked. Reheat the chip oil and deep-fry the chips again until they are golden and crispy.
Serves 4

FOR THE SUMMER PEA SALAD:
Whisk the thyme, lemon juice, oil and sugar together. Season to taste. Break the sugar-snap peas and toss with the other peas in the dressing.

1 tbsp freshly chopped thyme
1 tbsp lemon juice
1 tbsp groundnut oil
2 tsp sugar
Salt and black pepper to season
175 g (6 oz) sugar-snap peas
175 g (6 oz) fresh peas

FOR THE TARTAR SAUCE:
1 quantity mayonnaise (see page 183)
1 tbsp each of capers, gherkins, parsley and shallot, all finely chopped
½ tbsp lemon juice
Zest of 1 lemon
Salt and black pepper to season
Mix all the ingredients together and season to taste.

FOR THE TOMATO SAUCE:
2 tbsp shallots, finely chopped
1 red chilli, finely chopped
Little oil for cooking
3 tbsp tomato purée
Dash balsamic vinegar
1 tbsp water
1 tbsp sugar
150 g (5 oz) cherry tomatoes, quartered
Salt and black pepper to season

Fry the shallots and chilli in a little oil. Add the tomato purée, vinegar, water and sugar. Stir in the cherry tomatoes and season to taste.

Whole Lemon-roasted Sea Bream with a Leek and Quail's Egg Tartlet

Some people hate the idea of eating fish with the head still on. I love this as it reminds me of going abroad and choosing a fish from a tank, then it arrives a couple of minutes later, piping hot and looking slightly startled. The more substantial tartlet offsets the light sea bream nicely.

4 sea bream
50 g (2 oz) butter
1 lemon, thinly sliced
Salt and black pepper to season

Make three slashes on each side of the sea bream and rub the butter into the gaps. Place the fish on a baking tray and cover with the lemon slices. Season well and roast in the oven at 200°C / 400°F / gas mark 6 for 15 to 18 minutes or until cooked.

For the tartlets:
1 quantity shortcrust pastry (see page 183)
1 large leek, thinly sliced
Little olive oil
2 eggs
150 ml (¼ pt) double cream
Salt and black pepper to season
12 quail's eggs

Roll out the pastry thinly and use to fill four greased 10cm / 4 inch tartlet moulds. Freeze for 30 minutes then bake at 180°C / 350°F / gas mark 4 for 10 to 15 minutes or until just golden. Allow to cool and turn out. Sauté the leek in the olive oil until softened, and divide amongst the tartlets. Whisk the eggs with the cream and season. Pour over the leeks. Breaking 3 quail's eggs into the middle of each tartlet and bake at 200°C / 400°F / gas mark 6 for 10 to 15 minutes.
Serves 4

CITRUS-BAKED RED SNAPPER WITH A ST CLEMENT'S HOLLANDAISE SAUCE

Baking the fish in paper will help retain plenty of moisture. Hollandaise sauce is a pain to make — but the results are worth tearing a little bit of hair out for. If the sauce begins to curdle, make the base of the sauce again and gradually add the separated mixture instead of the butter.

4 whole red snapper
50 g (2 oz) butter
1 each lemon, lime and orange, thinly sliced
Salt and black pepper to season

Make three slashes on each side of the snappers and rub in the butter. Place each fish on a large sheet of greased greaseproof paper and cover with the fruit. Season well and pull up the paper, scrunching it well at the top to hold it together. Bake at 200°C / 400°F / gas mark 6 for 15 to 18 minutes.

FOR THE ST CLEMENT'S HOLLANDAISE:

3 tbsp white wine vinegar
8 black peppercorns
1 bay leaf
2 egg yolks
150 g (5 oz) butter
1 tbsp lemon juice
Finely grated rind of 1 orange and 1 lemon
Salt and black pepper

Simmer the vinegar, peppercorns and bay leaf until reduced by two-thirds. Set a heatproof bowl over a pan of simmering water. In the bowl whisk the egg yolks with the strained vinegar reduction until slightly thickened. Gradually whisk in cubes of the butter. Remove from the heat and whisk in the lemon juice and orange and lemon rind; season to taste. Serve immediately.
Serves 4

Marinated Tuna with a Lime and Grapefruit Salsa and Sesame Stir-fried Vegetables

I am usually reluctant to use strong flavours in seafood dishes but tuna can take them on well. You could use swordfish or shark instead, both of which have a good meaty texture.

4 x 175 g (6 oz) tuna
steaks
2 tbsp olive oil
Juice and finely grated
rind of 2 limes

2 tsp sugar
Salt and black pepper to
season

Place the tuna steaks on a dish and whisk together the other ingredients. Pour over the tuna and cover with cling film. Refrigerate for 4 hours. Fry the tuna steaks in a hot pan for a couple of minutes on each side. Pour over the marinade and cook for a further minute.

For the lime and grapefruit salsa:
2 segmented pink grapefruits
Juice and finely grated rind of 1 lime
2 tsp sugar
2 tsp olive oil
1 each red and green pepper, finely chopped
1 red chilli, finely chopped
Cut the grapefruit segments into small pieces and toss with the other ingredients.

For the sesame stir-fried vegetables:
1 tbsp vegetable oil
2 tsp sesame oil
450 g (1 lb) of mixed vegetables, including sugar-snap peas, baby corn, baby carrots and red onion
1 tbsp sesame seeds
1 tbsp soy sauce
Salt and black pepper to season

Heat both the oils in a wok or large pan and add the vegetables and stir fry to cook, making sure they are still crisp. Add the sesame seeds and soy sauce and cook for 1 minute. Season to taste.
Serves 4

dinner with juliet

TROUT IN FILO PASTRY WITH AN ORANGE, ALMOND AND BACON SAUCE

If the parcels are too fiddly, you could always roast the trout whole or poach the skinned fillets in the sauce. This recipe would also work well with Salmon or Artic Char fillets.

225 g (8 oz) raw carrot and courgette, cut into julienne strips
2 tbsp melted butter
4 sheets filo pastry
4 skinned trout fillets

Sauté the carrot and courgette strips in a little of the melted butter until slightly softened. Use most of the remaining melted butter to brush each sheet of filo pastry. Fold each sheet in half and butter the top. Divide the vegetables on to each sheet and place a trout fillet on top. Draw the pastry up to form a parcel. Brush with butter and place each parcel onto a greased baking sheet. Bake at 200°C / 400°F / gas mark 6 for 10 to 12 minutes or until golden.

FOR THE SAUCE:
8 thick rashers of unsmoked back bacon, cut into thin strips
600 ml (1 pt) orange juice
Zest of 1 orange
100 g (4 oz) butter
Salt and black pepper to season
3 tbsp flaked almonds, toasted

Fry the bacon until crispy. Add the orange juice and zest and boil until reduced by half. Whisk in the butter. Season to taste and add the toasted almonds.
Serves 4

meat

& game

dinner with juliet

Fillet of Scottish Beef with a Whisky, Cream and Grain Mustard Sauce

This sauce is so tasty but very simple to make if you are struggling for time. It pays to buy beef from a butcher and not a supermarket, as it will be hung for longer and be much more tender. This is probably the most popular main course in the restaurant. You can substitute the whisky for brandy, if preferred, but always use Scottish beef as it can't be beaten!

6 shallots
Little oil for cooking
300 ml (½ pt) whisky (I use Glenkinchie or Highland Park but a blended whisky like Famous Grouse also works well)
4 tbsp whole grain mustard
2 tsp brown sugar
900 ml (1½ pt) of double cream
Salt and black pepper to season
4 fillet steaks weighing approximately 225 g (8 oz)

Firstly make the sauce. Finely chop then fry the shallots in a little oil until golden. Add the whisky and boil rapidly until the liquid is reduced by two-thirds. Add the grain mustard, sugar and cream. Simmer until the sauce is thick enough to coat the back of a spoon. Season to taste. Remove from the stove and heat through gently when needed. In a very hot frying pan brown the beef well on all sides to seal the meat. Transfer to a hot oven (220°C / 425°F / gas mark 7) and cook for 4 minutes for rare, 10 minutes for medium and 15 to 20 minutes for medium/well done. After cooking allow the meat to rest in a warm place for 5 minutes. Serve with the hot sauce.
Serves 4

dinner with juliet

BRAISED SHIN OF BEEF WITH RED WINE AND CARAMELISED SHALLOTS

The flavour you get from beef shin is incredible. This dish should be eaten with crusty, warm bread to soak up the sauce.

1.1 kg (2½ lb) beef shin, cut into cubes
2 tbsp flour
900 ml (1½ pt) beef stock
300 ml (½ pt) red wine
150 ml (¼ pt) port
Salt and black pepper to season
8 shallots, peeled
50 g (2 oz) butter
2 tbsp sugar

Toss the meat in the flour until well coated, then brown well in a hot pan. Transfer to a good-sized pot and pour over the stock and red wine. Simmer gently for 1 hour or until the meat is very tender, by which time the flour should have thickened the gravy. Add the port and season to taste. Fry the shallots whole in the butter. Sprinkle over the sugar and cook until caramelised. Serve on top of the beef.
Serves 4

BEEF NORMANDY

This is my personal favourite beef dish. If you don't like the idea of using foie gras you can use any other livers for the pâté but the result will not taste as good. It is important to ladle the brandy into the pan and not pour it as the alcohol will ignite and turn the brandy bottle into a blowtorch! I made this mistake once and I now value my eyebrows more than ever.

110 g (4 oz) foie gras
Little oil for cooking
1 tbsp brandy
2 tbsp double cream
Salt and black pepper to season
1 onion
450 ml (¾ pt) red wine
450 ml (¾ pt) beef stock (see page 182)
25 g (1 oz) butter
25 g (1 oz) flour
1 tbsp port
4 beef fillets, weighing approximately 225 g (8 oz) each
4 disks of white bread, 2.5 cm / 1-in thick
Little olive oil for frying

First make the pâté. Sauté the foie gras in a little oil until the middle of the livers are not raw but just pink. Ladle the brandy into the pan and ignite. Allow the flames to subside and the liquid to boil to almost nothing. Purée in a food processor with the cream, until smooth. Season and set aside.

For the sauce, chop the onion and sauté until golden. Add the red wine and reduce by two-thirds. Add the stock and reduce by one-third. Melt the butter and mix in the flour. Whisk drops of this mixture into the red wine sauce until you have the desired consistency. Strain and discard the onions. Season to taste and pour in the port. Remove from the heat until needed.

In a hot frying pan seal each side of the steaks until well browned. Transfer to a high oven (220°C / 425°F / gas mark 7) for 5 minutes for rare, 10 to 15 minutes for medium or 20 minutes for well done. Fry the disks of bread in the olive oil until crisp and golden. Serve the steak on top of the croûton with some pâté on top. Pour over the sauce.
Serves 4

dinner with juliet

RACK OF LAMB IN AN ORANGE AND CAMPARI SAUCE

Ask your butcher to French trim the lamb for you as it can be quite fiddly to do yourself. It is difficult to judge whether a rack of lamb has been cooked to the preferred 'doneness'. Take it out of the oven when you think that it is nearly ready and cut into it to check how much longer it needs. Cooking times can also vary, depending on the thickness of the fat on the lamb. Campari may seem like an odd thing to put in a sauce but it offsets the sweetness of the orange well. If you really can't stand Campari, you can substitute Port, brandy or Armangnac.

4 racks of lamb, each with four ribs
Little oil for cooking
1 onion, finely chopped
150 ml (¼ pt) Campari
275 ml (½ pt) orange juice
275 ml (½ pt) beef stock
50 g (2 oz) butter
50 g (2 oz) plain flour
Finely grated rind of 2 oranges
2 oranges, segmented
Salt and black pepper to season

With a sharp knife, score the skin of the lamb in a lattice pattern. Heat a little oil in a frying pan and fry the lamb, skin-side down for about 2 minutes until it starts to brown. Seal the lamb on all sides, until the meat is lightly browned. Place the racks in a roasting tin, skin-side up and roast in the oven at 220°C / 425°F / gas mark 7 for 20 to 35 minutes depending on whether you like your meat pink or well done.

To make the sauce, sweat the onion in a little oil and add the Campari. Simmer for 2 minutes. Add the orange juice and stock and reduce by one-third. Strain off the onions. Melt the butter and mix with the flour. Whisk the roux into the sauce to thicken it. You might not need it all but use until the sauce covers the back of a spoon. Stir in the orange rind and segments. Season to taste.
Serves 4

LAMB SHANKS IN THEIR OWN GRAVY

The omission of herbs or other flavours in this recipe is no cop out. I don't think that the flavour that comes from the lamb shank can be improved on. Slow cooked meats need as much attention as cooking tender cuts. You have to be very careful not to overcook, as the meat will go stringy. If you get this right, the meat should be falling off the bone but still meltingly tender.

4 lamb shanks
1.2 litres (2 pt) beef stock (see page 182)
570 ml (1 pt) red wine
25 g (1 oz) butter, melted
10 g (½ oz) flour
Salt and black pepper to season
Freshly chopped parsley to garnish

In a hot frying pan, seal the lamb shanks on all sides. Put them in an ovenproof dish and pour over the stock, wine and a little water to cover them. Cover with a lid or tinfoil and bake at 190°C / 375°F / gas mark 5 for 1½ hours. At this stage check the lamb. It should be falling away from the bone and very tender. If it is not done put it back for another 15 minutes and keep checking until it is cooked. Do not let it over-cook.

To finish the gravy, strain into a pan. Mix together the butter and the flour and, over a low heat, gradually add to the gravy, whisking all the time, until thickened. Season to taste and serve poured over the lamb and sprinkle over the chopped parsley.
Serves 4

dinner with juliet

Lamb Noissetes in Marsala with Roast Peaches

Some people turn their noses up at lamb Noissetes but I think they are very tasty. You might have noticed by now that I use a lot of fruit in my savoury cooking, but why not? The only rule to cooking is that the results should taste good.

Little oil for cooking
8 lamb Noissetes
1 onion, peeled and finely chopped
150 ml (¼ pt) Marsala wine
450 ml (¾ pt) beef stock (see page 182)
3 tbsp apricot jam
Salt and black pepper to season
50 g (2 oz) butter
4 peaches

In a little oil, fry the lamb Noissetes on each side. Add the onion and cook over a low heat for 2 minutes. Add the Marsala, beef stock and apricot jam. Allow to boil and reduce until syrupy. If the lamb is cooked but the sauce is still too thin, remove the lamb and return to the sauce before serving. Season to taste. In a separate pan, heat the butter. Half and stone the peaches. Fry them in the butter and allow to brown. Transfer to a hot oven (220°C / 425°F / gas mark 7) for 5 to 7 minutes or until cooked.
Serves 4

Venison en Croûte with a Spiced Plum Sauce and Sautéed Wild Mushrooms

Venison is far more popular in the restaurant than beef, so it is reassuring to know that it is no longer associated with killing Bambi's mum. This sauce is quite Christmassy with the mulled wine spices. The strong-flavoured wild mushrooms are a good accompaniment to the robust venison.

4 shallots, peeled and chopped
Little olive oil for cooking
Bottle red wine
570 ml (1 pt) beef stock (see page 182)
450 g (1 lb) plums, halved and stoned
Pinch of cinnamon and mixed spice
25 g (1 oz) butter
25 g (1 oz) flour
Pinch of sugar
Salt and black pepper to season
1 venison fillet, at least 700 g (1½ lb)
4 sheets filo pastry
Little melted butter
275 g (10 oz) wild mushrooms

To make the sauce, fry the shallots in the olive oil. Add the red wine and reduce until thick and syrupy. Add the stock and the plums, and reduce by half allowing the plums to disintegrate into the sauce. Pass the sauce through a sieve and return to the pan. Add the cinnamon and mixed spice. Melt the butter and mix with the flour. Add to the sauce in small spoonfuls, whisking all the time, until the sauce has thickened. Add the sugar and season to taste.

To cook the venison, divide into four portions and, in a hot frying pan, brown well. Brush the filo pastry with the melted butter and wrap each piece of venison in one sheet. Brush the top of each parcel with melted butter. Transfer to a hot oven (220°C / 425°F/ gas mark 7) for 5 minutes for medium-rare or 10 to 15 minutes for medium to well done. Sauté the mushrooms in a little butter and season to taste.
Serves 4

GAME CASSEROLE WITH STILTON AND PARSLEY DUMPLINGS

Your game dealer will be able to recommend which game is in season. The choice of game you use will depend on how strongly flavoured you want the casserole to be. I usually use a mixture of venison, rabbit, hare and pigeon. The addition of port to the gravy is a lovely combination with the Stilton dumplings.

FOR THE DUMPLINGS:

175 g (6 oz) self-raising flour
75 g (3 oz) shredded suet
75 g (3 oz) Stilton, crumbled
2 tbsp freshly chopped parsley
Salt and black pepper

Mix the flour, suet, Stilton and parsley in a bowl and add the seasoning. Make a well in the centre and add a little water. With a spoon draw in the mixture, adding more water, if necessary, until you have a soft dough. Form into small balls.

FOR THE CASSEROLE:

700 g (1½ lb) stewing game, cut into cubes
Flour for dusting
Little olive oil for cooking
275 ml (½ pt) red wine
1.25 litres (2 pt) beef stock (see page 182)
Salt and pepper to season
2 onions, peeled and finely chopped
4 potatoes, peeled and quartered
4 large carrots, peeled and quartered
150 ml (¼ pt) port

Preheat the oven to 180°C / 350°F / gas mark 4. Toss the game in the flour then shake it to get rid of the excess. Fry the game in batches in the olive oil. Remove the last of the game from the pan and pour in the wine. Scrape the pan with a wooden spoon to deglaze. Place the game in a casserole dish. Pour over the wine and the stock and add a little salt and pepper. Fry the onions and add to the casserole. Cover and bake for 1½ hours. Add the vegetables and the port to the casserole and place the dumplings on the top. Return to the oven for 30 minutes or until the game is tender and the dumplings have risen.

Serves 4

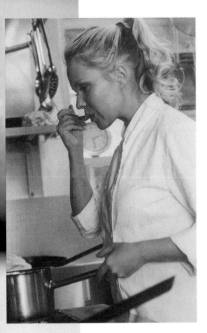

Pheasant Breasts with a Cream, White Wine and Grape Sauce

The chicken available nowadays is usually rather bland so pheasant is a tastier alternative. Use a mixture of red and green grapes to give the dish some colour.

Little oil for cooking
8 pheasant breasts
275 ml (½ pt) white wine
275 ml (½ pt) chicken stock (see page 182)
275 ml (½ pt) double cream
225 g (8 oz) red and green seedless grapes
Salt and black pepper to season

Heat a little oil in a pan and fry the pheasant breasts for a couple of minutes on each side until slightly browned. Pour over the wine and stock, and simmer for 20 to 25 minutes, until the breasts are cooked and tender. Remove the pheasants from the liquid and set aside. Boil the liquid until it has reduced by half. Add the cream and boil until the sauce coats the back of a spoon. Return the pheasant to the sauce with the grapes and warm through. Season to taste.
Serves 4

Duck in a Berry Sauce with Roasted Vegetables

Duck can vary greatly in flavour and tenderness so go for good quality, particularly if you like it pink in the middle. Forget the diet – keep the skin on as the flavour is superb. You can use the fat that the skin renders to make the roasted vegetables.

4 duck breasts with the skin on
275 g (10 oz) mixed berries
275 ml (½ pt) beef stock (see page 182)
Salt and black pepper to season

With a sharp knife, make close diagonal slashes into the skin of the duck. Place the duck, skin-side down in a cold frying pan. Put the pan on the heat and let it get very hot. Cooking the duck skin this way renders the most fat, making the skin really crispy. Fry for 3 minutes then turn the duck breasts over and fry on the other side for 3 minutes. Place the duck breasts in an ovenproof dish, skin-side up, and roast at 220°C / 425°F / gas mark 7 for 8 to 12 minutes depending on whether you like the meat pink or well done. Drain the fat from the pan and reserve. Add the berries and stock. Simmer until the sauce has thickened and season to taste. Add any juices the duck has rendered from the oven. Carve the duck into thin strips and arrange on the plates with the sauce.

For the roasted vegetables:
4 large carrots
4 potatoes
1 leek
Reserved duck fat
Salt and black pepper to season

Peel the carrots and potatoes and, with the leeks, cut into chunks. Toss in the duck fat and place on a baking tray. Roast in a hot oven (220°C / 425°F/ gas mark 7) for 25 to 30 minutes until cooked and browned. Season to taste.
Serves 4

SPATCHCOCKED QUAIL WITH THYME, LEMON AND BUTTER

This recipe is ridiculously simple yet it looks very impressive for a dinner party. This dish is also very nice served cold for summer picnics. Quails and poussin can vary in size and sometimes you may need 2 per portion.
I generally like garlic to be a subtle taste but if you are a garlic freak then add as much as you want – chances are I'll end up sitting next to you in the cinema, as usual!

4 quails or poussin
2 cloves of garlic, finely sliced
75 g (3 oz) butter
2 tbsp finely chopped thyme
Finely grated rind and juice of 2 lemons
2 tbsp olive oil
Salt and black pepper to season

Remove the backbone from each bird by cutting down each side with a pair of kitchen scissors. With a sharp knife, cut small slits in the skin of both legs and breasts. Stuff the garlic, butter, thyme and lemon rind between the skin and meat. To get them open, press down on the breastbone; and to keep them flat, skewer diagonally across the body. Place on a roasting tray and drizzle with the lemon juice and olive oil. Season well then place in a hot grill for 15 to 20 minutes, turning them occasionally.
Serves 4

Glazed Ham with a White Leek Sauce

When I was in outside catering I used to make glazed hams like they were going out of fashion. I have included this recipe because I think that everyone should know how to cook a ham. I know that white or béchamel sauce is quite old-fashioned but I sometimes prefer it to a cream sauce and it goes perfectly with the ham. I have given you a quantity of ham that will serve more than four people, but it is worth having the extra for sandwiches and salads. If you have never cooked your own ham before, you will find it hard to go back to the pre-cooked variety as the flavour is out of this world.

1 ham, weighing approximately
2kg (5 lb)
570 ml (1 pt) cider
1 onion
2 carrots

10 black peppercorns
6 tbsp honey
Grated rind of 2 oranges
Cloves for studding the ham

Put the ham in a large pot and cover with cold water. Bring to the boil. Remove the ham from the pot and pour away the water. Rinse the pot well and return the ham to it. Pour over the cider. Half the onion and the carrots and add to the pot with the peppercorns. Cover the ham with water and bring to the boil. Simmer, covered for 1½ hours. Remove from the water. Preheat the oven to 190°C / 375°F / gas mark 5. Remove the skin from the ham but leave as much fat on as possible. Make scores in the fat to form a diamond pattern. Mix the honey and orange rind and rub into the ham. Place the ham in a roasting tin and stud the ham with cloves. Roast in the oven for 20 to 25 minutes or until the fat has turned brown and started to crisp

For the white leek sauce:
50 g (2 oz) butter
50 g (2 oz) plain flour
570 ml (1 pt) milk
1 leek
Oil for frying
Salt and black pepper to season

In a heavy-based saucepan, melt the butter then add the flour and stir over a medium heat until it starts to foam. Add one-quarter of the milk. Allow the milk to heat through without stirring then whisk in. Repeat this process in stages until all the milk is used then stir the sauce over the heat until it reaches the desired consistency. Fry the leeks in a little oil until they have softened and add them to the sauce. Season to taste.

Serves 4

vegetarian

dinner with juliet

WILD MUSHROOM RISOTTO WITH CHESTNUTS

Risotto is a great supper dish and should be cooked, glass of wine in hand, while having a good moan to your loved one about what a terrible day you've had. Once you have mastered risotto-making you can experiment with all sorts of different flavours. Try sun-dried tomatoes and basil or summer pea and lemon.

2 tbsp olive oil
3½ oz butter
450 g (1 lb) wild mushrooms
150 g (5 oz) roast chestnuts
4 shallots
225 g (8 oz) Arborio rice
900 ml (1½ pt) white wine
900 ml (1½ pt) vegetable stock (or chicken stock for non-veggies) (see page 182)
50 g (2 oz) buffalo mozzarella, grated or finely chopped
Salt and black pepper to season
Freshly chopped parsley and Parmesan shavings to garnish

Melt the oil and 2 oz butter in a large pan. Add the mushrooms and chestnuts and sauté until they are lightly browned. Remove from the pan and set aside. Chop the shallots finely and add to the pan with the rice. Stir for a minute so that the shallots are softened and the rice is well coated in the oil and butter. Add the wine and boil until there is only a tablespoon of liquid remaining. Add half the stock and simmer until the rice has absorbed almost all the liquid. Keep adding a little stock until the rice is cooked. The risotto should be creamy and not too dry. Stir in the rest of the butter with the mozzarella, mushrooms and chestnuts. Season to taste and sprinkle over the chopped parsley and Parmesan to serve.
Serves 4

POTATO GNOCCHI WITH SPINACH AND PARMESAN

As gnocchi is quite heavy, I only serve it as part of a meal with plenty of crispy salad on the side. If you are not partial to spinach, you could always use watercress, tomatoes or sautéed wild mushrooms in its place.

700 g (1½ lb) floury potatoes
2 eggs, beaten
225 g (8 oz) plain flour
1 onion
Little olive oil
1 clove garlic, crushed

150 ml (¼ pt) white wine
275 ml (½ pt) double cream
1 egg yolk
Handful spinach leaves
3 tbsp grated Parmesan
Salt and black pepper to season

Boil the potatoes in their skins until tender but not mushy – they should not soak up too much water. Peel the potatoes and finely grate. Place the grated potatoes onto a clean work surface and make a well in the centre. Pour in the beaten eggs and sprinkle on half of the flour. Mix with your hands. Try to make a light dough, so do not over-knead the mixture. Add more flour until the dough holds together but is still light. You may not need all the flour.

Shape the dough into long rolls, 2.5cm / 1 inch in diameter and cut into 2.5cm / 1 inch pieces. Place in a greased dish and cover with cling film until needed.

Chop the onion and sauté in a little olive oil until softened and golden. Stir in the garlic and add the wine. Reduce by half and add all but one tablespoon of the cream. Mix the leftover cream with the egg yolk and whisk into the cream and wine mixture. Stir over a low heat until thickened but do not allow to boil. Stir in the spinach leaves and Parmesan and season to taste. Bring a large pan of salted water to the boil and poach the gnocchi, a few at a time. Cook until they rise to the surface of the water. Place the gnocchi in a serving dish and pour over the sauce. Grill under a high heat for a couple of minutes then serve hot and bubbling at the table.
Serves 4

GRATIN OF ROAST BUTTERNUT SQUASH WITH BRIE AND ALMONDS

This is one of my mum's favourite dishes that I cook. It is ridiculously simple but very tasty, too. I like to use Brie cheese but mozzarella also works well. In the restaurant we serve this with asparagus that has been lightly poached in a pan of water with a couple of tablespoons of sherry.

2 large butternut squash
Olive oil for drizzling
Salt and black pepper to season
175 g (6 oz) Brie
275 ml (½ pt) double cream
4 tbsp flaked almonds

Cut the squash in half and scoop out the seeds. Drizzle each half with olive oil and season well. Wrap each half in tinfoil and place on a baking sheet. Bake at 220°C / 425°F / gas mark 7 for 30 minutes or until the flesh is soft and tender. Remove the foil and scoop out the flesh. Slice the Brie and mix with the squash flesh. Check the seasoning. Put the squash and Brie back into the squash skins and drizzle over the cream. Scatter the flaked almonds on top and bake for a further 10 minutes.
Serves 4

Mediterranean Vegetable Gratin

This recipe is almost like vegetarian lasagne but without the pasta and a lot simpler. When cooking with tomato and especially tomato purée, it is always a good idea to add sugar as it will bring out the flavour of the tomato beautifully.

1 aubergine
4 plum tomatoes
1 each green, red and yellow peppers
1 red onion
4 tbsp tomato purée
1 clove garlic, crushed

1 tbsp sugar
2 tbsp red wine
6 basil leaves
Salt and black pepper to season
2 buffalo mozzarella
150 ml (¼ pt) double cream

Slice the aubergine, tomatoes, peppers and red onion. Whiz the tomato purée, garlic, sugar, red wine and basil. Season to taste. Layer the tomatoes, peppers and onions in an ovenproof dish and pour over the tomato sauce and top with half the cheese. Layer the aubergine on the top and pour over the cream. Finish with a layer of mozzarella. Bake at 190° C / 375°F / gas mark 5 for 20 minutes or until the vegetables are tender and the top has browned.
Serves 4

BLINI WITH ASPARAGUS, POACHED EGG AND HOLLANDAISE

This is a kind of bizarre version of Eggs Benedict with lovely soft eggs and hollandaise – and it is the ultimate hangover cure. Working chef's hours means that I get a hangover in the afternoon, not the morning, and this is the recipe I use to revive myself with an Alka Seltzer on the side.

110 g (4 oz) self-raising flour
Salt and black pepper to season
1 egg
110 ml (4 fl oz) milk
25 g (1 oz) butter, melted
25 g (1 oz) butter (refrigerated)
2 tbsp olive oil
8 asparagus spears
4 eggs
Hollandaise sauce to taste (see page 184)

Sift the flour and sprinkle on some salt and pepper to season. Make a well in the flour and drop in the egg and a little of the milk. Stir in with a whisk, pulling in the flour, adding more milk until you have a smooth batter that coats the back of a spoon. Stir in the melted butter.

Heat a little of the refrigerated butter and oil in a small frying pan and pour in some batter to coat the base of the pan. Fry until the batter begins to set. Loosen the edges with a pallet knife and turn the blini over. Fry on the other side until both sides are browned. Repeat until you have 4 blinis. Cover the blinis in tinfoil and keep warm in a low oven. Steam the asparagus till just cooked. Simmer some salted water and poach the eggs. Serve each blini with 2 spears of asparagus with a poached egg on top and spoon over the hollandaise sauce.
Serves 4

dinner with juliet

MIXED VEGETABLE TEMPURA WITH CHILLI AND GINGER DIPPING SAUCE

Oil for deep-frying
2 large carrots, cut into thin strips
2 courgettes, thinly sliced
12 baby corn
110 g (4 oz) sugar-snap peas
Salt to season

FOR THE BATTER:
175 g (6 oz) plain flour
2 egg yolks
450 ml (¾ pt) water
Pinch of salt

Heat the oil in a deep-fat fryer or in a heavy-based saucepan until a cube of bread sizzles when dropped in. Mix together the batter ingredients. The batter should be lumpy. Dip the carrots, courgettes, baby corn and sugar-snap peas in the batter and fry in batches. Drain on kitchen paper and season with a little salt.

FOR THE DIPPING SAUCE:
2 each red and green chillies
6 tbsp ginger syrup from a jar of stem ginger
2 tbsp soy sauce
2 tsp sesame oil
2 tbsp shredded spring onions

Chop the chillies and whisk together with the other ingredients. Serve with the tempura for dipping.
Serves 4

dinner with juliet

Happy

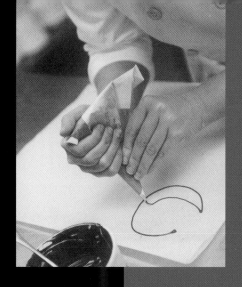

ever
afters

THE BEST ADVICE I HAVE EVER BEEN GIVEN IS DON'T LEARN FROM YOUR OWN MISTAKES – LEARN FROM OTHER PEOPLE'S.

dinner with juliet

HAPPY EVER AFTERS

The best advice I have ever been given is: Don't learn from your own mistakes – learn from other people's. If you fancy yourself as a restaurateur, here are a few tips from someone who has been to the edge and back.

The first thing you need is money – the more the better. You might be in a better financial prospect than I was but always try to get more finance than you think you will need. The main reason for this is that unexpected costs always come up that you didn't budget for. It's getting the finance that is difficult, not spending it. A restaurant eats money like a sponge soaks up water. Even the music you play comes at an annual fee; somehow I doubt if the old man from Cuba who sings on our favourite CD sees any of it.

You will have to draw up a business plan and a year's projection of profit-and-loss figures. You won't have any idea how much or little money you are going to make in your first year but don't worry – all you have to do is make up any figures you fancy while thinking 'this is a total waste of time.' When you are trying to sell the concept of your restaurant – in order to win over the opinion of a bloke whose shirt and tie doesn't match – is when you will begin to have the urge to drink more than usual. The early signs are a warning, you know.

If time wasting isn't your thing, then don't waste

that time trawling round every high street bank: they are all the same, no matter what promises they make. Don't ever expect your bank manager to understand the way your business works or what problems it brings you. During the hard times your bank will be about as helpful to you as a brick tied to your foot when drowning. Expect little and don't be disappointed.

Most people think that owning a restaurant is a real hoot and a thoroughly glamorous lifestyle. I won't say what I think of this but the word begins in 'b' and ends in 't'. When you are in the gathering-your-finance stage be prepared for some of your friends to offer an investment for a 'silent partnership'. To you a silent partnership might mean that they are investing the money, hoping to get some dividend back on it while staying out of the way. To them it means bringing in their friends all the time, not paying for anything and giving you their fourpeneth on everything you do while you do all the hard work.

I am glad that I didn't go down this route, as I know others that have regretted it deeply. If your friends tell you how to run your business when they have never run a business themselves, do what I do and staple their eyelids to the floorboards until they shut up.

When it comes to finance be prepared for things to get worse before they get better. In your first year,

don't be surprised if your staff get paid more than you do. This is totally unfair but so is life – get used to it. If you want to succeed, you're going to have to swallow your pride every now and then. If you are struggling to pay a bill, most people will be happy if they get some now and the rest later. This is a concept that many of my married, female friends are familiar with.

Many restaurateurs will tell you that making money is not their prime concern. Oh yeah? The more money you are making, the more successful you are and you don't want an unsuccessful business unless failure is your style.

So now that you've got a bit of cash to spend it's time to find your premises. You could either do what I did and start the whole thing from scratch or buy an existing restaurant business. Although this is contrary to my own experience, I would go for the existing business. This is for several reasons. Firstly, people already know the premises as a restaurant and will come to see what you have done with it. If the restaurant has a good reputation then getting finance will be a lot easier.

Even if the existing restaurant has a completely different set-up from what you envisage there are still advantages. You won't have to get permission to turn the place into a restaurant and it will already be licensed. I had to open without my licence and allow

IF YOU WANT TO SUCCEED, YOU'RE GOING TO HAVE TO SWALLOW YOUR PRIDE EVERY NOW AND THEN

dinner with juliet

people to bring their own wine, losing me a lot of income. I had thought that this would be a good way of getting people in to try the restaurant but I wonder if those people ever do return once you have your licence.

You will probably have to redecorate but providing you don't make any structural changes, you need never deal with the council planning department and take it from me – you don't want to.

Even if you are leasing the property of an existing business, you will have to pay a premium for buying the lease. This might seem like a lot of money but the chances are that your set-up costs would be more. You would get your business opened sooner too, giving you a better opportunity of getting some of that money back.

Most restaurants that fail in their first year are often very good restaurants but whose owners have made one of two mistakes. Either choosing a bad location or spending all their money on pointless things and not leaving any as a back up.

Location is everything. You could have the most beautiful restaurant in the world, the loveliest staff and food of the gods but if your restaurant is in the wrong area of town people won't come to it. There was a restaurant in Edinburgh that had a great reputation for good food but overlooked the red-light

MOST RESTAURANTS THAT FAIL IN THEIR FIRST YEAR ARE OFTEN VERY GOOD RESTAURANTS BUT WHOSE OWNERS HAVE MADE ONE OF TWO MISTAKES

district and eventually had to close. You might think that with the Scottish parliament up and running it would be full every night but sadly not. Although my restaurant isn't in a prime spot, it is in a lovely, vibrant area with plenty of nice bars surrounding it so people can come to the area for a whole night out, not just a meal.

You know as well as I do that the food is the most important thing but if you have got this far you probably have a good idea of what kind of food you want to serve. One thing that has worked very well with my menu is that the food is cooked in a sympathetic way. By that I don't mean that we stroke the fish and say sorry before we fry them. I mean that we let good produce speak for itself rather than trying to pile several flavours into one dish. One of the best things that I did was pay a lot of attention to my desserts, as so many restaurants let themselves down on the last course.

When you choose your suppliers, buy locally where possible. When somebody asks me where I get my seafood, I can tell them that it's from Armstrong's, on Raeburn Place, which is a stones throw from the restaurant. Customers like this because they don't feel that their food has come from a warehouse. A local supplier will treat you better and give you a more personalised service, allowing you to serve the best produce. Also, the kind chaps in your local shops will often do you the kindness of chatting you up when you go in. Believe me, with the lack of social life that your new venture will give you, you will be very grateful for this. But not that grateful…

Until you build up a reputation for your food, people will have no idea what it will taste like until they take their first bite so it is the image of the restaurant that will bring them in. You might want your restaurant to be the trendiest place in town and for a while it might be — until the next hip place comes along. An important thing to remember is that high fashion dates fast. I chose to go for a classic-contemporary look that has served me well; it will never date but still looks modern. If you are going for the minimalist approach, make sure you have good heating, as there is nothing worse than sitting in a cold-looking place that is actually cold.

You might want to get an interior designer or architect to do your interior for you. If you have no imagination of your own then go ahead. Remember, however, that whatever budget you give them, that is how much they will spend so you won't be making any savings. My father and I designed the interior of my restaurant and successfully achieved the look I really wanted, rather than the look a designer thought I wanted. My best piece of advice is to go for carpets instead of stone or wooden floors. Carpets give an instant feeling of comfort and eliminate the 'clomp, clomp, clomp' factor. Cosy lighting is another must as most restaurants could be improved ten-fold if they had warmer lighting.

Good lighting will also flatter your customers' appearance and with a bit of subtly sexy music will result in a more 'goin' on' Barry White, type of atmosphere. Lets just say that romantic surroundings result in couples having a few more brandies then a taxi for two, if you know what I mean. All in all, everyone's a winner.

Now you need your staff. Many a restaurateur will harp on about how wonderful and dedicated their staff are. It is important to remember that your staff are working for you because it suits them, and that is fair enough. You would be naive to think that your staff care half as much about your business as you do. I have been lucky and managed to keep my good

dinner with juliet

142 · desserts — happy ever afters

members of staff for a long time but the good ones are hard to find. I have always chosen my waiting staff, not for experience but for having a friendly personality. Waiting tables is a difficult job so a nice demeanour makes all the difference to the customers' enjoyment. Never encourage a 'them and us' feeling between the kitchen and front of house. I have never allowed a chef to shout at the waiting staff or each other.

I would seriously advise anyone opening a restaurant (if they are not already a chef) to learn to cook. Chefs can have a tendency to throw tantrums,

walk out in the middle of a busy night, turn up drunk or not turn up at all. You have to be prepared if this happens. I have always made a point of treating my staff well. I never lose my temper with waiting staff or the kitchen staff. I have begun to wonder if some of my chefs would have preferred me to shout and swear at them; many seem to believe that this is the way a kitchen works. Well, not in my kitchen it doesn't. A bad atmosphere in the kitchen seeps into the dining room. Try to create a happy working environment and when your staff have done a good job — tell them.

Being a boss has many disadvantages. What's the

fun in hiding in the cellar, having a cigarette when you are only hiding from yourself? What is the point in stealing stationary when you will be the one who has to replace it? It is a great thing to be in charge and have things the way you want them but this brings its own set of problems. Any aggravation amongst your work force is your responsibility to sort out. I try to treat my staff the way I would want to be treated and would like to think of myself as firm but fair.

Even this attitude does not always work out. As a young female boss, I have had male employees speak to me in a way that they would never dream of addressing an older male employer. Never put up with this. As the owner of a business you are the only person who cannot hand in their notice and get another job. Sacking somebody is a horrible thing to have to do, no matter how much they deserve it but you will have to do it at one point. I can put up with a lot of things but having an unhappy workplace isn't one of them. You will spend so much time at work, so make it as enjoyable as you can.

In this hypothetical restaurant in the sky, you now have premises, a gang of merry staff, food to sell and are not bankrupt yet. Let the customers roll in.

Customers are great. They make pay-days possible and allow you to pay your bills. So if you don't like (or can't handle) dealing with the public then the

restaurant trade isn't the one for you. Customers will have demands that range from the unreasonable to the downright bizarre. They can range from the loveliest people to the spawn of Satan – but you will need them all.

Lets start with the bad customers. You will get people in your restaurant who will be rude to the staff, pretend they know more about wine than they actually do and generally behave in an inconsiderate manner to all involved, not to mention each other. This type of person usually believes that the staff and the owner of a restaurant are impressed with this kind of behaviour. Well let me tell you that we are not impressed one bit. What they are trying to show you is that they go to restaurants all the time and your wonderful food and service is what they are used to. In reality this kind of person probably eats out once a year and has chosen you to host their annual misery fest. Smiling and being absurdly pleasant to them annoys them more than letting them get to you.

I have only had to throw one customer out who was being extremely nasty to a waitress. My staff know that they have to put up with bad manners from time to time and can handle difficult customers very well. You have to draw the line somewhere, however and as the owner you will be the one who has to deal with a difficult and potentially embarrassing situation.

YOUR GOOD CUSTOMERS WILL MORE THAN MAKE UP FOR THE BAD

The glove puppet can help in less extreme situations and certainly beats running out of the kitchen, meat cleaver in hand. Getting blood out of white linen can be very difficult, in my experience.

Your good customers will more than make up for the bad. Seeing the same people come back time after time because they enjoy your restaurant is a brilliant feeling. Always make sure that you recognise your regulars and offer them a complimentary liqueur with their coffee to make them feel special. In the same way, always treat first time customers in a special way and put yourself out to make them happy. Every regular customer has to pay a first visit.

My regular customers like the fact that my staff are so friendly. I encourage them to go for polite but cheerful service. One thing we will never do to our customers is put the napkins on their laps for them. I feel that this is intrusive and was probably started by some French Maitre'd as a way of getting a look at the customer's cleavage or groin, depending on which way he was inclined.

Somebody once asked me if I wanted my restaurant to be full of young, trendy, beautiful people. Nice thought but if you've ever walked down the street you might have noticed that not many people exist that fit this category. I am perfectly happy to have my restaurant filled with cheerful, satisfied customers, thank you very much.

You should be pleased with yourself by now. You are starting to build up a good reputation and word of mouth is getting around. So why don't we put a cog in the wheels? At some point, like it or not, your going to get the food critics in.

Whoever does the photography for food critics' by-line photos should receive an award because they rarely resemble their image in the newspapers. Think along the lines of at least three stones heavier, ten years older and further down the line when good looks were being dished out. Many food critics are honest people who will write an accurate account of

IF YOU EVER MANAGE TO MAKE YOUR WAY DOWN TO STOCKBRIDGE, A WARM WELCOME AND A GOOD MEAL AWAITS YOU

their visit to your restaurant. There are some, however who will think nothing of writing a vitriolic, sarcastic piece about you, full of untruths. This has happened to me once and I am fully convinced that it was because the critic in question had a problem getting his fat derrière into his seat.

It's lovely to get a good review but along with the bad they make no difference at all to how busy your restaurant is. You may find this surprising but the kind of person who spends their time reading restaurant reviews doesn't get out enough. If you get a bad review file it in the bin and get on with life. You can eventually get your revenge by running a successful restaurant and perhaps go on to writing a cookbook.

If none of the previous problems I have mentioned, put you over the edge, then the amount of calls from people trying to sell you advertising, will bring you pretty close. Take it from me, they get pretty miffed when you tell them where to stick their advertising. When times are hard, you can at least console yourself with the fact that you don't sell advertising space for a living.

As I am coming to the end of my tale, you might be wondering if that one (tenth) drink too many, that made me decide to have a restaurant, was worth it? I can honestly say that if I had known how tough it was going to be, I would have thought twice about becoming a restaurateur. I can now say that it was the right way to go. Every minute of the journey has taught me a lot and I now feel that if I can create a restaurant like mine, then the world truly is my oyster (mornay, of course).

I hope that I have dispelled some of the myths about the restaurant trade. Yes the journey is hard but this means that reaching your destination is all the more satisfying. The best thing about owning a restaurant is the satisfaction of seeing people eating the food that I have cooked and enjoying the surroundings and atmosphere that I created. It has been one hell of a roller coaster ride but the ups and downs have been worth every minute.

If you ever manage to make your way down to Stockbridge, a warm welcome and a good meal awaits you.

If you are still thinking of opening a restaurant of your own or are happy to remain a customer in one, please feel free to steal some of these recipes and pass them off as your own. Flattery will get you everywhere.

desserts

dinner with juliet

Fig, Berry and Marsala Trifle with Almond Macaroons

A good trifle cannot be beaten, and this recipe is the Ferrari of trifles. I use sherry a lot in my cooking but for desserts I tend to prefer Marsala as it has a softer, more *puddingy* taste. In the restaurant we serve this dessert with lemon parfait (see page 178).

4 figs
4 tbsp raspberries
275 ml (½ pt) canned, mixed berries in their juice
2 tbsp lemon juice
½ quantity vanilla sponge (see page 187)
4 tbsp Marsala
2 egg yolks
50 g (2 oz) castor sugar
½ tbsp cornflour
150 ml (¼ pt) milk
275 ml (½ pt) double cream

Quarter the figs and divide among four glasses with the raspberries. Purée the canned berries with the lemon juice and pour over the fruit. Soak the sponge in the Marsala and place on top of the fruit. To make the custard, whisk the egg yolks, sugar and cornflour with a little of the cold milk. Boil the rest of the milk and pour over the egg mix, whisking all the time. Put the custard back into the pan and stir over a low heat until thickened. Pour over the trifles and chill until set. Whisk the cream until it forms stiff peaks and pipe on to the trifles.

For the Almond Macaroons:
110 g (4 oz) ground almonds
50g (2 oz) flaked almonds
75g (3 oz) castor sugar
2 egg whites

Preheat the oven to 180°C / 350°F / gas mark 4. Mix the ground almonds, flaked almonds and sugar in a bowl. Whisk the egg whites till they form stiff peaks and, using a large metal spoon, fold into the dry ingredients. Spoon small drops of the mixture on to a greased baking sheet and bake for 12 to 15 minutes or until golden.
Serves 4

TIRAMISU WITH CHOCOLATE BISCOTTI

I used to think that tiramisu had become a bit passé; however, it still proves to be a highly popular dessert and really is a modern classic. So many people make tiramisu badly, and it is often too dry and tasteless. All trifles should be moist and boozy, and Tiramisu is a trifle, an Italian trifle, but a trifle all the same – a point you should make very clearly if anyone over 80 is to eat it.

250 g tub mascarpone cheese
150 ml (¼ pt) double cream
2 tbsp icing sugar
150 ml (¼ pt) Amaretto liqueur
½ quantity vanilla sponge (see page 187)
150 ml (¼ pt) strong espresso coffee
Cocoa powder for dusting

Mix the mascarpone with the double cream. Sift in the icing sugar and, using a large metal spoon, fold in with the liqueur. In a bowl, dip the sponge in the coffee, squeezing it slightly so that the sponge soaks up the coffee well. To assemble, layer the sponge with the cream mixture and dust with cocoa powder to finish.

FOR THE CHOCOLATE BISCOTTI:

4 eggs
140g (4½ oz) castor sugar
275g (10 oz) self-raising flour
1 tsp baking powder
1½ tbsp cocoa powder
50g (2 oz) flaked almonds
75g (3 oz) dark chocolate drops

Beat the eggs and sugar until pale, thick and fluffy. Sift the flour, baking powder and cocoa into the egg mix and, using a large metal spoon, fold in with the almonds. Cover the dough with cling film and refrigerate for 20 minutes. Divide the dough on to a greased baking sheet in three long rolls. Cover with cling film and refrigerate for a further 20 minutes. Bake at 180°C / 350°F / gas mark 4 for 20 minutes. Allow to cool then slice each roll diagonally into thin strips. Lay the strips flat on the baking tray and bake for a further 5 minutes each side. Cool on a wire rack and store in an airtight tin.

Serves 4

MANGO AND PINEAPPLE PUDDING WITH CARAMEL AND BRANDY SAUCE

With this pudding recipe you could substitute almost any soft fruit you want. Berries, plums and peaches all work well. Our customers are always asking how we make this sauce. The method is so ridiculously simple that I am almost ashamed!

218 g condensed milk
150 ml (¼ pt) double cream
2 tbsp brandy
2 mangoes
1 small fresh pineapple
125 g (4½ oz) butter
125 g (4½ oz) sugar
2 eggs
125 g (4½ oz) self-raising flour

Remove the label from the tin of condensed milk and pierce a hole in the top. Sit in a pot and fill with water 2.5cm / 1 inch below the top of the tin. Bring to the boil then allow to simmer for 1½ hours, making sure the water is topped up as it evaporates. Remove the tin from the water and allow to cool. The condensed milk will have thickened and turned a caramel colour. Whisk together with the cream and brandy. The sauce can be reheated later in a pan, over a gentle heat.

Preheat the oven to 180°C /350°F / gas mark 4. Remove the fruit from the mango and pineapple and cut into small cubes. Beat together the butter and sugar until pale and fluffy. Gradually whisk in the eggs. If the mixture begins to separate, add a little of the flour and it will come together. Sift in the flour and fold using a large metal spoon. Fold in half of the fruit. Brush four small bowls or one big one with melted butter and line the base(s) with greaseproof paper. Put the remaining fruit in the bottom of the pudding bowl(s) then fill with the pudding mix. Bake for 20 to 25 minutes or until well-risen and slightly browned on top. A skewer inserted into the pudding should come out clean. Run a knife round the edge of the pudding(s) and invert onto a plate to serve immediately. Alternatively they can be allowed to cool in the pudding bowl(s) and turned out later. To reheat, microwave them on full power for 30 seconds, loosely covered with cling film.

Serves 4

CHOCOLATE AND STEM GINGER PUDDINGS WITH WHITE CHOCOLATE AND GLAYVA SAUCE

This is a dessert for the more sophisticated palate and was inspired by my love for chocolate covered stem ginger. Glayva is a spicy liqueur and perks up a white chocolate sauce nicely.

175 g (6½ oz) sugar
175 g (6½ oz) butter
3 eggs
150 g (5 oz) self-raising flour
40 g (1½ oz) cocoa powder
1 level tsp baking powder
8 pieces stem ginger, roughly chopped

FOR THE WHITE CHOCOLATE AND GLAYVA SAUCE:
100g bar white chocolate
150 ml (¼ pt) double cream
2 tbsp Glayva liquer

Preheat the oven to 180°C / 350°F / gas mark 4. Beat the sugar and butter together until soft and fluffy. Gradually beat in the eggs, adding a little of the flour if the mixture starts to separate. Sift in the flour, cocoa and baking powder and fold in using a large metal spoon. Fold in one-third of the stem ginger. Brush four small pudding bowls or one large one with butter. Line the base(s) with a disk of greaseproof paper.

Put the remaining ginger into the bottom of the pudding bowl(s), then fill with the pudding mix and bake for 20 to 25 minutes or until well risen and a skewer inserted comes out clean. Run a knife round the puddings and invert onto a plate. Alternatively, allow to cool in the pudding bowl(s) before turning out. Reheat in the microwave for 30 seconds at full power, covered loosely with cling film.

To make the sauce, break the white chocolate into a heavy-based saucepan and pour over the cream. Stir over a gentle heat until the chocolate is melted and stir in the Glayva. Pour the chocolate sauce over the hot puddings and serve.
Serves 4

EXOTIC FRUIT PAVLOVA

This is a perfect summer dessert, which is lovely and light.
Meringues can be a bit of a hassle to make, as they have to sit
for ages in a very low oven. For this reason I have spread the
meringue mix quite thin and built up the Pavlovas in layers. This
exotic fruit version is my favourite but I also love to use berries
and put a tablespoon of whisky in the cream for a Scottish
version.

2 egg whites
110 g (4 oz) castor sugar
Oil for greasing
450 ml (¾pt) double cream
3 tbsp icing sugar
3 tbsp liqueur (Cointreau and Malibu work well with the
exotic fruits)
3 passion fruit, seeds and juice removed
1 mango, peeled and sliced
8 lychees, peeled and sliced
2 kiwi fruit, peeled and sliced

Preheat the oven to 130°C / 250°F / gas mark ½. In a clean,
dry bowl, whisk the egg whites until they form stiff peaks. Add
a tablespoon of the sugar and whisk vigorously until it is totally
incorporated. Keep adding the sugar this way, one tablespoon
at a time. Do not be tempted to add the sugar too quickly as
this will make the mixture runny. If you want to be sure that
you have mixed the meringue correctly, hold the bowl upside
down above your head. If the mixture sticks to the bowl, you
have done it right!

Brush the oil on a layer of greaseproof paper and place on a
baking sheet. Spread the meringue in thin disks, 10cm / 4 inches
in diameter on the greaseproof paper. Bake in the oven for 30
to 40 minutes. Remove and allow to cool, then peel from the
greaseproof paper.

To make the Chantilly cream, whisk the cream until it forms soft
peaks. Sift in the icing sugar and pour in the liqueur. Fold
together using a large metal spoon. To assemble the Pavlovas,
layer the meringue, the fruit and the cream three times.
Serves 4

Baked Alaska

I seldom see this dessert in restaurants anymore, which is a shame. In my restaurant we pour a ladle of flaming brandy over the Alaska as we serve it. Edinburgh must be a city of pyromaniacs because when people see the flames they all want a baked Alaska too. You can use almost any combination of ice creams but I like to use an ice cream and a sorbet.

225 g (8 oz) vanilla sponge (see page 187)
2 tbsp brandy
300 ml (½ pt) lemon sorbet (see page 179)
450 ml (¾ pt) strawberry ice cream (see page 178)
3 egg whites
175 g (6 oz) castor sugar

Place squares of the sponge onto a baking tray to form a circle shape. Drizzle with brandy, reserving one tablespoon for flambéing. Spoon a layer of sorbet on top of the sponge then a layer of ice cream. Try to form an upside-down cone shape with the ice cream and sorbet. Whisk the egg whites until they form stiff peaks then gradually whisk in the sugar. Cover the Alaska with the meringue, ensuring there are no holes and that the ice cream is sealed in. Place the Alaska in the freezer until you need it. This can be made the day before. Just before serving, bake the Alaska at 220°C / 425°F / gas mark 7 for 5 to 7 minutes or until the meringue is starting to turn golden. At the table, carefully heat the remaining brandy in a heatproof metal ladle over a low flame (such as a candle) then allow to light and pour over the Alaska.
Serves 4

dinner with juliet

GRAND MARNIER SOUFFLÉS

This recipe was created for a wedding party of 40 where the groom insisted on having Grand Marnier soufflés for the dessert. I remember standing by the oven praying that they would rise. In the end they rose so much that they were huge, and the waiting staff managed to serve them with military precision so that everyone had their dessert at the same time.

3 egg yolks
150 ml (¼ pt) orange juice
2 tbsp flour
2 oranges, segmented and the rinds finely grated
3 tbsp Grand Marnier
6 egg whites
150 g (5 oz) castor sugar
Butter for greasing

Preheat the oven to 220°C / 425°F / gas mark 7. In a pan, whisk the egg yolks, orange juice and flour together. Stir over a low heat until thickened to a white sauce consistency. Stir in the orange segments and rind and Grand Marnier. Whisk the egg whites until they form stiff peaks and gradually whisk in the sugar. Using a large metal spoon, fold one-third of the egg white mix into the orange sauce and then gently fold in the rest. Divide into four greased ramekins and sit in an ovenproof dish with 2.5cm / 1 inch of water. Bake for 8 to 10 minutes or until risen and golden.
Serves 4

CHOCOLATE SOUFFLÉS

For many women this is the perfect dessert as it is super light but dangerously chocolatey. You have got to use a dark bitter chocolate with at least 70 per cent cocoa solids. I like to slit the top of the soufflé and pop in a ball of vanilla ice cream. Admittedly, working off this indulgence in the gym the following day is less enjoyable.

200g (7 oz) dark chocolate (at least 70 per cent cocoa solids)
3 egg yolks
2 tbsp flour
6 egg whites
75 g (3 oz) castor sugar
Butter for greasing

Preheat the oven to 220°C / 425°F / gas mark 7. In a heatproof bowl set over a pan of simmering water, melt the chocolate. Remove from the heat and whisk in the egg yolks and flour. In a clean bowl, whisk the egg whites until they form stiff peaks. Gradually whisk in the sugar. Fold one-third of the egg white mix into the chocolate mixture then, using a large metal spoon, fold in the remainder gently. Grease four ramekins with the butter and fill with the soufflé mix. Run a knife round the edges to ensure they rise evenly. Place the ramekins in an ovenproof dish with 2.5cm / 1 inch of water. Bake for 10 to 12 minutes or until well risen. Serve immediately.
Serves 4

MULLED WINTER FRUITS

This is a good dessert for anyone who is trying to stick to a low-fat diet or is glucose intolerant. When choosing your fruit go for the firmer ones, as they will hold together when they are poached.

4 pears
1.2 litre (2 pt) red wine
110 g (4 oz) castor sugar
1 tbsp cornflour
4 figs
2 plums
175 g (6 oz) grapes

Peel the pears, leaving the stems on and cutting the bottoms off so that they stand up. Place them in a saucepan and cover with the red wine and sugar. Bring to the boil then allow to simmer for 20 minutes or until the pears are tender. Remove the pears and reduce the wine by half. Mix the cornflour with a little cold water until it is smooth. Add this to the wine reduction, whisking all the time until the wine is syrupy. Cut the stems off the figs and score the tops then squeeze the base of them slightly so that they open out. Half and stone the plums. Put the pears back into the red wine sauce with all the other fruits and heat through gently until the plums, figs and grapes have softened slightly.
Serves 4

Choux Pastry Swans in a Berry River

Everyone is terrified of choux pastry but it is really not that hard if you get the textures right at the various stages of mixing. This recipe can be used for any size of choux bun or éclair but I think that these swans look cool.

100 g (3 oz) butter
300 ml (½ pt) water
150 g (5 oz) plain flour
4 eggs
300 ml (½ pt) double cream

4 tbsp icing sugar
2 tbsp Cointreau
225 g (8 oz) mixed berries
Juice and finely grated rind of 1 lemon

Preheat the oven to 200°C / 400°F / gas mark 6. Place the butter and water in a saucepan and heat gently until the butter is melted. Bring to the boil and pour in the flour. Remove from the heat and beat with a wooden spoon until the mixture is smooth and only just begins to come away from the edge of the pan. Allow to cool for 20 minutes.

Gradually beat in the egg until the mixture becomes smooth and glossy. Place two tablespoons of the mixture into a piping bag and pipe 8 'S' shapes on a greased baking sheet. These will make the swans necks. Set aside.

Spoon the rest of the mixture on to a separate, greased baking tray to form eight oval balls. Bake for 20 to 25 minutes until risen and golden. Slit the tops to allow the air to escape and bake for a further 2 minutes. Allow to cool.

Bake the 'S' shapes for 5 minutes, until crispy and golden. Whip the cream until it forms soft peaks and, using a large metal spoon, fold in 2 tablespoons of the icing sugar and the Cointreau. With a sharp knife, cut an oval shape from the top of each choux bun and then cut the disk in half lengthways. Hollow out the bun and fill with the Chantilly cream. Stick the oval halves in the cream to form the wings and an S shape for the neck.

To make the berry sauce, heat the berries, the remaining icing sugar and the lemon juice and rind in a pan with 2 tablespoons of water. Pass through a sieve and drizzle on the plates, sitting the swans on top.
Serves 4

Strawberry and Passion Fruit Crème Brûlée with an Exotic Fruit Salsa

Many people judge a restaurant on their crème brûlée, and I have always thought it bizarre that standards should be measured on such a simple dish. It is often the case, however, that it is the simple things that many chefs make a mess of.

150 g (5 oz) strawberries
4 passion fruit
3 egg yolks
40 g (1½ oz) castor sugar
Finely grated rind of 1 lemon
275 ml (½ pt) double cream
3 tbsp castor sugar to finish

For the exotic fruit salsa:
1 mango
2 kiwi fruit
1 papaya
8 physallis fruit
2 tbsp lime juice

Preheat the oven to 180°C / 350°F / gas mark 4. Hull and quarter the strawberries. Half and scoop out the fruit of the passion fruit. Divide the fruit between 4 ramekins. Whisk the egg yolks, sugar and lemon rind until pale and thick. Boil the cream and pour over the egg mixture, whisking all the time. Pour into the ramekins and sit them in an ovenproof dish with 2.5cm / 1 inch of water. Bake for 20 to 25 minutes until they are just set. Remove from the water bath and allow to cool. Sprinkle with the castor sugar and either grill or blowtorch until the sugar is melted. Allow the sugar to cool for a couple of minutes before serving. To make the salsa, finely chop the fruits and toss with the lime juice.
Serves 4

dinner with juliet

BREAD AND BUTTER PUDDING

Ten years ago we would have been laughed out of town if we had put bread and butter pudding on the menu but now it is fashionable again. Although I have stuck to the traditional dried fruits I have soaked the fruits in booze and added some dried apricots. If possible, use stale bread rather than super fresh, as this will give better results. Serve with cream or ice cream.

2 tbsp dried, chopped apricots
2 tbsp sultanas
2 tbsp raisins
1 tbsp mixed peel
4 tbsp brandy
2 eggs
75 g (3 oz) castor sugar
150 ml (¼ pt) double cream
150 ml (¼ pt) milk
50 g (2 oz) butter
5 slices white bread
1 tbsp icing sugar

Soak the fruit in the brandy overnight. Preheat the oven to 180°C / 350°F / gas mark 4. Whisk the eggs and sugar together until pale and fluffy. Beat in the double cream and milk. Butter the bread. Layer the bread, fruit and egg mixture in a heatproof bowl, finishing with a layer of bread and egg mixture. Place the pudding bowl in a roasting tin, half-filled with water, and bake for 35 to 45 minutes or until the custard is just set and the top is browned and crusty. Dust the top of the pudding with icing sugar and grill until the sugar has caramelised.
Serves 4

CREPE SUZETTE

This dessert has a sense of occasion about it and I always
think it turns out better if I am wearing an evening dress
when I am cooking it.

110 g (4 oz) plain flour
40 g (1½ oz) castor sugar
Zest of ½ orange
Zest of ½ lemon
1 egg
275 ml (½ pt) milk
40 g (1½ oz) melted butter
Extra butter for frying

In a bowl, mix the flour, sugar and zests. Make a well in the
centre and drop in the egg. Start to beat the egg and add the
milk in a steady stream, beating all the time and pulling in
the flour to form a smooth batter. Stir in the melted butter.

Melt a little butter in a frying or crepe pan if you have one.
Pour a little of the batter into the pan and swirl to coat the
base of the pan. Fry for about 2 minutes or until the batter
begins to become firm. Loosen the edges with a pallet knife
and flip the crepe over or toss if you are brave! Fold into a
quarter shape and place on a warm dish and cover with foil.
Repeat until you have eight crepes.

FOR THE SAUCE:
75 g (3 oz) castor sugar
4 tbsp orange juice
110 g (4 oz) butter
Juice and zest of 1 lemon
4 tbsp Grand Marnier
4 oranges, segmented
2 tbsp brandy

In a frying pan, over a gentle heat, melt the sugar in 2
tablespoons of the orange juice. Add the butter and swirl
until it has melted into the sugar. Add the rest of the orange
juice, lemon juice and zest and Grand Marnier. Stir until the
sauce is well mixed and has a glossy appearance. Transfer the
crepes into the pan with the orange segments and coat with
the sauce. Heat through and pour over the brandy and
carefully ignite.
Serves 4

ICE CREAM

VANILLA SEMIFREDDO

2 egg yolks
Seeds from 1 vanilla pod
150 g (5 oz) castor sugar
350 ml (12 fl oz) double cream
4 egg whites

Whisk the egg yolks, vanilla and sugar together until thick and pale. Lightly whip the double cream and, using a large metal spoon, fold into the egg yolks. Whip the egg whites until they form stiff peaks and fold gently into the other mixture. Line a baking tin or mould with cling film and spoon in the mixture. Freeze for at least six hours.

VARIATIONS

Fold in 110 g (4 oz) grated dark chocolate and 4 tablespoons of coffee liqueur when you fold in the cream.
Fold in 110 g (4 oz) toasted, flaked almonds and 4 tablespoons of Amaretto liqueur when you fold in the cream.
Layer the finished semifreddo in the mould with some melted jam or lemon curd.

STRAWBERRY ICE CREAM

6 egg yolks
75 g (3 oz) castor sugar
400 ml (14 fl oz) milk
550 g (1¼ lb) strawberries, hulled and quartered
2 tbsp lemon juice
75 g (3 oz) icing sugar
450 ml (¾ pt) double cream

Whisk the egg yolks and castor sugar together with a little of the milk until pale and thick. Bring the rest of the milk to the boil, then pour into the egg mixture in a thin stream, whisking all the time. Return to the pan and stir over a low heat without boiling until the consistency is of custard. Simmer the strawberries with the lemon juice, icing sugar and a little water until soft. Stir into the custard. Either churn in an ice cream maker or freeze for 2 hours, whisking the mixture every 30 minutes. Once semi-frozen, stir in the cream and freeze again for 2 hours.

LEMON PARFAIT

175 g (6 oz) castor sugar
Juice and zest of 3 lemons
3 egg whites
570 ml (1 pt) double cream

Place the sugar and lemon juice and zest in a pan and add enough water to cover the sugar. Heat gently until the sugar has dissolved, then simmer until the syrup has reached the soft ball stage (a drop of the syrup should go solid but not hard when dropped into a saucer of cold water). Whisk the egg whites in a clean bowl until they form stiff peaks. Continue to whisk adding the syrup in a thin stream until it is all incorporated. Keep whisking until the mixture is cool and thick. Whisk the cream until it forms stiff peaks and fold the two mixtures together using a large metal spoon. Pour into a large bowl or individual moulds and freeze for at least 2 hours.

VARIATIONS

Replace half the lemon juice with orange or lime juice.

LEMON SORBET

570 ml (1 pt) lemon juice
275 ml (½ pt) water
150–225g (5–8 oz) castor sugar
Finely grated rind of 3 lemons
2 egg whites

In a pan, over a low heat, dissolve the lemon juice, water and 75g /
3 ounces of the sugar with the lemon rind. Taste the liquid and add
more sugar if the juice tastes very bitter. Either churn the liquid in
an ice cream maker or freeze for 2 hours, whisking every half an
hour. Once the mixture is frozen but still soft, whisk the egg whites
and gradually whisk in the remaining sugar. Using a large metal
spoon, fold the meringue into the sorbet and return to the freezer.

CHOCOLATES

DARK CHOCOLATE AND WHISKY TRUFFLES

225 g (8 oz) highest quality dark chocolate
225 ml (8 fl oz) double cream
3 tbsp whisky
400 g (14 oz) highest quality dark chocolate to coat
Gold leaf

Melt the chocolate and stir in the cream and whisky. Chill until set and roll into balls. Melt the coating chocolate and dip the truffles. Dry on greaseproof paper. Decorate with flecks of gold leaf.

WHITE CHOCOLATE, APRICOT AND ORANGE TRUFFLES

75 g (3 oz) dried apricots
4 tbsp Cointreau or Grand Marnier
225 g (8 oz) white chocolate
150 ml (¼ pt) double cream
75 g (3 oz) flaked almonds
2 tsp orange zest
400 g (14 oz) white chocolate to coat
Blanched almonds to decorate

Chop the apricots and soak overnight in the liqueur. Melt the chocolate and stir in the cream, apricots, any liqueur that has not been soaked up, almonds and orange zest. Refrigerate until set and roll into balls. Melt the coating chocolate and dip the balls, then dry on greaseproof paper. Decorate with blanched almonds.

DARK CHOCOLATE, CHERRY AND CASSIS TRUFFLES

110 g (4 oz) canned cherries, drained and chopped
3 tbsp Cassis
225 g (8 oz) highest quality dark chocolate
225 ml (8 fl oz) double cream
400 g (14 oz) highest quality dark chocolate to coat
3 tbsp cocoa powder

Soak the cherries in the cassis overnight. Melt the chocolate and stir in the cream, cherries and cassis. Refrigerate until set and roll into balls. Melt the coating chocolate, dip the balls and then roll in the cocoa powder.

CHRISTMAS PUDDING TRUFFLES

75 g (3 oz) mixed, dried fruit
3 tbsp brandy
225 g (8 oz) highest quality dark chocolate
225 ml (8 fl oz) double cream
400 g (14 oz) highest quality dark chocolate to coat
110 g (4 oz) white chocolate to decorate
Small mint leaves to decorate

Soak the dried fruit in brandy overnight. Melt the chocolate and stir in the cream, fruit and brandy. Chill until set and roll into balls. Melt the dark coating chocolate and dip the balls. Place on greaseproof paper to dry. Melt the white chocolate and drizzle over to make the chocolates look like wee Christmas puddings. Decorate with mint leaves.

BASIC RECIPES

BEEF STOCK

2 kg (4½ lb) beef bones, if possible include
marrow bones
2 onions, peeled and quartered
4 carrots, peeled and roughly chopped
1 leek, trimmed and roughly chopped
15 black peppercorns
1 tbsp tomato purée

Preheat the oven to 200°C / 400°F / gas mark
6. Wash the bones to remove any blood and
place with all the other ingredients, except the
tomato purée, in a roasting tin. Roast for 20
minutes. Rub the tomato purée into the bones
and return to the oven for 5 minutes. The
vegetables should be browned at this point. Put
all the ingredients into a large pot and bring to
the boil. Simmer for 3 hours, skimming off any
scum that forms. Strain the stock through a fine
sieve and reduce if a stronger flavour is
necessary.

CHICKEN STOCK

1 uncooked chicken, weighing about 2 kg
(4½ lb)
2 onions, peeled and quartered
1 leek, trimmed and roughly chopped
15 black peppercorns

Put all the ingredients in a pot and cover with
cold water. Bring to the boil and simmer for 2
hours, skimming off any scum that forms on the
top. Strain through a fine sieve and reduce if
necessary.

VEGETABLE STOCK

3 onions, peeled and quartered
3 leeks, trimmed and roughly chopped
4 large carrots, peeled and roughly
chopped
1 head of celery, roughly chopped
20 black peppercorns
Few fresh parsley stalks

Place all the ingredients in a pot and cover with
cold water. Bring to the boil and simmer,
covered, for 40 minutes. Strain through a fine
sieve and reduce if necessary.

Fish Stock

2 kg (4½ lb) white fish bones
1 leek, trimmed and roughly chopped
1 onion, peeled and quartered
1 lemon, halved
15 black peppercorns

Place the ingredients in a large pot and bring to the boil. Simmer for 10 minutes, skimming off any scum that forms. Take off the heat and leave to stand for 20 minutes before straining through a fine sieve.

Shortcrust Pastry

75 g (3 oz) butter
175 g (6 oz) plain flour
Pinch of salt

Rub the butter into the flour and salt. Add cold water, a little at a time, and knead lightly until you have pliable elastic dough. Refrigerate until needed.

Mayonnaise

2 egg yolks
1½ tsp English mustard
1 tsp sugar
150 ml (¼ pt) olive oil
150 ml (¼ pt) vegetable oil
½ tbsp lemon juice
½ tbsp white wine vinegar

In a bowl, whisk the egg yolks with the mustard and sugar. Mix the two oils together and whisk half into the yolks very gradually. When you have used half of the oil, whisk in the lemon juice and white wine vinegar. Resume whisking in the oil until you have the desired thickness.

HOLLANDAISE SAUCE

Hollandaise sauce can be very tricky. If it begins
to separate, add a dash of very cold water and
whisk vigorously to bring back together.

2 tbsp white wine vinegar
2 tbsp water
Sprig of fresh tarragon
1 tsp black peppercorns
350 g (12 oz) unsalted butter
5 egg yolks
Salt and black pepper to season

In a pot, boil the vinegar, water, tarragon and
black peppercorns and reduce by half. Strain and
set aside. Melt the butter and separate the clear
butter from the white whey. Discard the whey.
Sit a stainless steel bowl over a pan of
simmering water. Add the egg yolks and with
half of the vinegar reduction until the mixture
froths and begins to become thick. Add the
butter very gradually, whisking all the time.
When you have added almost all of the butter,
taste the sauce and add more of the vinegar
reduction to taste. Whisk in the remaining butter
and season the sauce. Cover the bowl and stand
in a warm, not hot place. If the sauce needs
reheating when you are ready to serve it, whisk
it over simmering water.

DAUPHINOISE POTATOES

8 large potatoes, peeled and sliced
450 ml (¾ pt) double cream
150 ml (¼ pt milk)
1 large onion, sliced
Salt and black pepper to season

Place the potatoes, cream, milk and onion in a
large pan and bring to the boil. Simmer until
the potatoes are cooked. Season to taste,
transfer to a heatproof dish and place under a
hot grill until browned on top.

POTATOES BRAVADOS

8 large floury potatoes, peeled
4 tbsp olive oil
Salt and black pepper to season

Cut the potatoes into small cubes. In a bowl toss
them with the olive oil. Place on a baking sheet
and drizzle over any oil that is left in the bowl.
Season with the salt and pepper and bake for
30 minutes or until golden and crispy.

Oatmeal Potatoes

75 g (3 oz) butter
4 tbsp oatmeal
8 peeled and boiled new potatoes
Salt and black pepper to season

Melt the butter in a pan. Add the oatmeal and stir over a low heat to heat through and cook the oatmeal slightly. Add the potatoes and stir to coat in oatmeal and butter. Season to taste.

Lemon Dressing

150 ml (¼ pt) groundnut oil
150 ml (¼ pt) lemon juice
Grated rind of 1 lemon
3 tbsp castor sugar
Black pepper to taste

Whisk all the ingredients until the sugar is dissolved.

Scottish Oatcakes

200 g (7 oz) oatmeal
Pinch baking soda
½ tsp salt
½ tsp pepper
25 g (1 oz) butter
100 ml (4 fl oz) water

Preheat the oven to 180°C / 350°F / gas mark 4. Mix the oatmeal, baking soda, salt and pepper in a bowl. Melt the butter and add to the oatmeal with the water. Mix well to form a moist dough. Sprinkle some oatmeal on a clean surface. Divide the dough into three pieces and gently roll out to form rough circles. Cut each circle into quarters and gently place each piece on a well-oiled baking sheet. Bake for 10 minutes and then turn over and bake for a further 10 minutes. Allow to cool and store in an airtight container until needed. Oatcakes are best eaten warm so if you are making them ahead, put them in a hot oven for a minute before serving.

BREAD

2 tsp dried yeast
450 g (1 lb) strong white bread flour
1 tsp salt

Fill a jug with one-third of water – it should be hand hot (half cold and half boiling water). Sprinkle on the yeast. Stir, then leave in a warm place for 5 minutes or until the yeast has gone foamy on the top. Sift the flour and the salt in a large bowl, make a well in the centre and pour in the yeast and water. Stir to bring in the flour, adding more water until you have a soft, pliable dough. Transfer on to a floured surface and knead for about 10 minutes, until the dough is very elastic and smooth. Place in a greased bowl and cover with a tea towel. Leave in a warm place for 1½ hours or until doubled in size. Knock back the dough with your fist and leave to rest for 5 minutes. Shape the dough into two long rolls or several small rolls. Place on a greased baking sheet and cover with oiled cling film. Leave to rise once more until doubled in size. Bake at 220°C / 425°F / gas mark 7 for 35 to 40 minutes or until risen and golden. The bread should sound hollow when tapped on the bottom.

VARIATIONS

Knead 110 g (4 oz) stoned olives, 110 g (4 oz) sun-dried tomatoes and 110 g (4 oz) feta cheese into the dough before shaping into loaves.

Knead in the grated rind of two oranges and 3 tablespoons of walnut oil at the first kneading stage.

Before shaping the dough, roll it flat and spread it with pesto then roll up before baking.

Melba Toast

Makes 16 triangles

4 slices medium cut, square white bread

Toast the bread, either in a grill or a toaster, until both sides are crispy and golden. Cut the crusts off and slice the bread in half through the middle. Cut each thin slice diagonally in half and place under the grill, uncooked side up, until crispy and golden.

Vanilla Sponge

You can make as much or as little sponge as you like by using the same weight in all the ingredients. Weighing the eggs first, and then making sure that the butter, sugar and flour are exactly the same quantity, eliminates the mistakes that can be made by using eggs that are too small or big.

5 eggs
Same weight butter
Same weight sugar
Same weight self-raising flour.
½ tsp vanilla essence

Beat the butter, sugar and vanilla together until light and fluffy. Whisk in the eggs one by one. Sift in the flour and, using a large metal spoon, fold in lightly. Spread the mix into a greased and lined 24cm / 9½ inch baking tin or on a baking sheet. Bake at 180°C / 350°F / gas mark 4 for about 20 minutes or until risen and golden.

Variations

Add the grated rind of one lemon, lime, orange or even grapefruit to the mix at the first stage.

Replace one-third of the flour with cocoa powder and half a teaspoon of baking powder.

TIPS FOR SUCCESSFUL COOKING

It may seem obvious but read the whole recipe through before you begin as a certain type of dish or equipment may be needed that you do not have.

When cooking with alcohol, particularly wine, you will get better results if you use spirits or wine of a good quality. A bad tasting wine will make a bad tasting sauce so using the Liebfraumilch that Aunty Maureen gave you for Christmas in 1985 won't be a good idea.

When following recipes use either metric or imperial measurements, never both. When measuring, spoons are level and eggs are medium.

Some of the recipes contain raw eggs. This should be avoided if you are ill, pregnant, elderly, a small child, or frightened of raw eggs.

Unless otherwise stated, always use double cream. Butter is always lightly salted even in dessert recipes.

Again, unless otherwise stated, all herbs are

fresh and black pepper is freshly ground. If possible use Malden Sea Salt as you get a better flavour but if you only have normal salt, the world will not come to an end.

All recipes in this book serve four, except when otherwise stated.

Ovens are strange creatures that often have a mind of their own, especially if you are baking several things at once. In some of the recipes the fish and meat that you use may vary in size and quality, which will affect the cooking times. For this reason I have allowed some variation in baking and cooking times. It is often a good idea to check the contents of your oven a couple of minutes before the baking time is up. When cooking sauces, the time it takes for the sauce to reduce will vary on the size of your pan.

Food usually tastes better if the person cooking is enjoying it. I get much better results if I am having fun in the kitchen rather that cooking on sufferance. A glass of wine helps greatly it has to be said.

INDEX

dinner with juliet

OTHER TITLES FROM LOMOND

THE SCOTCH WHISKY BOOK
Tom Bruce-Gardyne
Hardback £15
ISBN 1 84204 021 9

SCOTTISH COOKERY
Christopher Trotter
Paperback £5
ISBN 1 84204 024 3